"This is a powerful story that graphically illustr [ ] and especially young men, of the absence of a fa[ ] our young people have no father figure and the results are disastrous! We know the absolute importance of a caring adult in every child's life. Young men with no father figure in their lives are at great risk in the world. They must have an adult to model themselves on and who provides guidance in their lives. We at America's Promise Alliance are working to help young people graduate from high school, ready to take the next step to prepare them for the work force. We stress the importance of that caring adult in a young person's life. Someone who cares; someone to listen; someone who has faith in you. It gives the individual a strength to over come the in equities that life brings. It is the key to success.

—ALMA POWELL, Chair, America's Promise Alliance

John Turnipseed's story shows how a changed heart will shift what you think of your self and the impact you can have. I thank God for you, John Turnipseed, for sharing your story, for allowing Jesus to change your heart, and for you deciding to love and lead others to be the best they can be. I'm calling all the John Turnipseed-types forward. Let the shifting begin. It is time to change the world, your state, your city, your community, your hood, your street, your family, and your life. But it starts with you. Go all in and finish the race. We all need you."

—SHAUN ALEXANDER, NFL MVP, award-winning author of *Touchdown Alexander* and *The Walk*

"Based on his tragic, troubled background, it's a miracle John Turnipseed is where he is today. His story is a clear example of the power of fathers—the chaos that happens when they drop the ball, the blessing that comes when they do what's right, and most of all, the healing found in the arms of the heavenly Father. You will be inspired by John's story: his courage to rise above his circumstances, his teachable spirit, and his ultimate surrender to a God who is greater than all the troubles and shortcomings in our lives.

—CAREY CASEY, CEO, National Center for Fathering

"I am drawn to stories of people overcoming adversity. Stories of the human spirit rising above and conquering over the struggles, hardships, and downright hell and we all encounter at some point during our life's journey. This is what attracted me to John's story and the reason I wanted to play his part in the Turnipseed movies. Hearing, reading, and seeing these types of stories motivate me to keep fighting and to keep the faith when I go through struggles. If you are at all like me, then just one chapter of John's life will do the same for you."

—LAWRENCE GILLIARD, Jr., American Character Actor and Hollywood Movie Actor

"I starting reading this book and couldn't stop. What a powerful and well-written story. The story of John Turnipseed is one that should be read and deeply studied by all who have a call to the transformation of urban lives and communities. John Turnipseed's trials, testimony, and transparency shed a bold light on the historic and present challenges facing too many urban, under-resourced, and high-risk families. There is still much work to be done to address the pain and violence connected to so many fatherless young men. This story inspires me to stay the path of the transformation, healing, and empowerment of the urban poor and disenfranchised."

—EFREM SMITH, President/CEO of World Impact
Author of *The Hip Hop Church* and *The Post-Black and Post-White Church*

"It is far easier to lock up and put away criminal offenders than to understand the root causes of their behavior and offer them a path of redemption. In this enormously relevant and personal story, John Turnipseed openly utilizes his own historic, egregious behavior to guide the reader to those root causes and then offers that redemptive path. *Bloodline* offers great hope for transformation of our prisons."

—JAY BENNETT, Chairman, *Halftime*

"This is a powerful story of transformation about a man convicted in flesh by his sins yet redeemed in spirit by a conviction from Christ. Thank you Mr. Turnipseed for this amazing testimony of redemption. Your life provides hope to all of us that second chances are possible when we accept the healing grace of God."

—DR TOM BLEE, HealthPartners

"One lives life forward and understands it backwards. This book decodes a life truly transformed. For many, their lives speak volumes. John's life roars with unspeakable adversity and amazing perspective. A must-read for anyone seeking insight and true wisdom."

—PHIL STYRLUND, CEO, The Summit Group

"John Turnipseed is a living witness and example of the transformational power of Jesus Christ. John's life experiences have made him an excellent candidate to speak into the life and brokenness of our communities due to the cycle of crime and culture of rebellion. One of the things that I have come to admire about John is his commitment to his family. Because John's heart is to see people restored, his bloodline runs deeper than his family of origin. Through his work at the *Center for Fathering*, John has added members to his family countless beyond number. He has become a father to many, a brother to others, and a source of inspiration to all who know him."

—QUOVADIS MARSHALL, National Director,
Restorative Church Coalition of Prison Fellowship Ministries

"John Turnipseed's powerful story reminds us that no person is beyond salvation—no matter how desperate or deplorable his life and no matter for how long. When he found God, he also found forgiveness, hope, and purpose; moreover, his life has become an inspirational example of redeeming faith, love of family, and a passionate commitment to serving others. *Bloodline* shows us that it's not only possible to break the cycle of poverty, crime, and despair in successive family generations, it's also necessary to do so, for the sake of all our children now and yet to come."

—BILL MILLIKEN, Founder of Communities In Schools
and Author of *From the Rearview Mirror*

"*Bloodline* by John Turnipseed is an important read in understanding a portion of our society. Some families and communities are a breeding ground for a life of crime. Twenty-five percent of all the incarcerated people in the world are right here in the United States. John Turnipseed was a criminal, serving time in juvenile and adult institutions. He honestly and bravely lays out his whole criminal record and his much later spiritual, moral, and behavioral renewal during his change to a man of integrity and responsible citizenship.

"John is my friend of many years. It hurts to read those experiences of his criminal years since I know him only in the years in which he has yielded himself to the sanctifying grace of Jesus Christ. I have watched the impact of Art Erickson's loving skills ever since John came to Urban Ventures. From this book you might share my revulsion of his confession of his criminal life in community and in state penal institutions.

"Who is at fault? Will others come to my conclusions? I will name two; the fathers and the penal institutions themselves.

"Here is an enlightened account by a person who has gone through it all as a criminal leader and is now an honest, outgoing leader in his community—reaching out to lead others, young and older, into righteousness and responsibility. Read and answer this question: Can you forgive and encourage such a person as John Turnipseed?"

—AL QUIE, Minnesota Congressman
and Governor

"When I was a police officer with the Minneapolis Police Department, I knew John Turnipseed during his life of crime. He remembers that I arrested him once. Decades later, Turnipseed has expressed gratitude to all law enforcement officers for holding him accountable for his actions. He values the consequences he received.

"I now serve as Sheriff of Hennepin County and my agency operates the largest jail in Minnesota. I reached out to Turnipseed to create a class that teaches life skills for inmates in the jail. The inmates respect Turnipseed and embrace his message because he speaks with raw honesty about his darkest days and his path toward positive change. People who are incarcerated—and anyone who has faced tremendous challenges—will be inspired by Turnipseed's life story. He turned away from bad choices and a troubled past and found a way to make his struggle meaningful so that others can transform their lives as he has."

—RICHARD STANEK, Hennepin County Sheriff

"*Bloodline* is a story that is so common in communities where their residents have been excluded from the primary economy of the nation. It is a riveting account, almost a playbook, for how to entrap generations in a prison system from which few actually recover. It's a must-read to understand what happened and how we stop the useless depletion of families that are essential to creating a future that is inclusive to all. This book deals boldly with the American tragedy of empty family, broken community, and a spiritual collapse that occurs when "fathering" is replaced by...crime and hopelessness!"

—JOHN THOMPSON, former Urban Ventures Board Chair and retired SVP and GM at Bestbuy.com

"Everyone needs to read this book. Through a combination of true urban-life realities, and then truly thoughtful reflections, the reader is given the opportunity to hear about positive change through perseverance, hope through adversity, and grace for a second chance that then gets worked out in daily existence. This book is a must-read for anyone who wants to make a powerful and significant difference in their community, city, and world."

—DR. DAVID HILLIS, Leadership Foundations, President

"John Turnipseed is one of those rare and extraordinary people in life whose early upbringing and influences would predict a tragic and failed life. Instead John was transformed and has dedicated his life to helping and saving (yes, saving) other men and families. He has a huge heart, genuine humility, and exceptional wisdom. Read this book and be amazed at what God has wrought and John has done.

—JOEL JENNINGS. CHAIRMAN, Gopher Sport

"John Turnipseed, #102556, was incarcerated by the State of Minnesota until 1989. He heard God calling him in his cell at the Stillwater Prison and has become what we hope will be the result of incarceration—a person who can flourish, despite the obstacles in front of him. I recall the day John came back to the cell block at the prison to film part of his story. Surely this was the last place he expected to see again. Seeing John there that morning reminded me of the story in Luke 15 of the prodigal son. John's story is an excellent example of what can be done by those who are ready to move forward with their lives in a positive, productive manner."

—John R. King, Former Warden, Stillwater Prison

"Tom Skinner often said: 'Before we hear the Good News we must hear the bad news.' And an African proverb says, 'When the nest is broken, the birds are lost!' Multiple generations of fatherless families have produced huge burdens on society, families, and children. We have lost our fathers, now losing our mothers, lost our kids, lost our families, and we are losing our culture. This marriage implosion and disappearance of the intact family produces broken kids and broken neighborhoods. We do not have just a youth problem; we have an adult problem. We have created a cradle-to-prison pipeline and grown a prison industry with 2.4 million inmates.

"There is a deep need to understand the dynamics of what has produced our multi-generational poverties in cities, on reservations, and now in our suburbs and culture. Father absence is endemic at every level of our society. This book on the life of John Turnipseed is essential to understanding these problems and the need for intervention and mentoring over a long period of time—all this combined with a *changed* heart, a *transformed* mind, a *healed* hurt, *equipped* hands, and a hope *restored* on the part of each participant. It will also document the importance of developing what John calls the need for an internal 'character math,' which he later expands to a 'character curriculum.' Sensitize yourself to the bad news, seek your own changed heart and transformed mind, then building on the resources, let us begin plans for a marriage explosion of healthy, intact families with early childhood learning and education; high school, college, and trade school graduations; and dynamic and vibrant communities once again.

—Art Erickson, StudiOne-Eighty, Urban Ventures

"Remarkable, riveting, forceful. *Bloodline* is the true story transformation of a career criminal, pimp, and drug addict, John Turnipseed. It is the triumph of one man's journey through the pits of hell in the streets, prisons, drugs and violence to sobriety, hope, inspiration and salvation.

"I grew up with John Turnipseed and I watched his personal transformation and witnessed its impact on thousands of young men who struggle in and out of prisons, without hope, without jobs and without faith, without a moral compass. John's belief that everyone can turn their life around no matter the circumstances is an inspiration for all of us working on the front lines to change the conditions for African-American men and their families.

"I was reintroduced to John in 1999 after not seeing him for many years. What I witnessed was nothing short of a miracle. At that time, I was the director of planning and development for Hennepin County, Minnesota, working on a project to address the significant problems of facing African-American men in our community. John learned about what I was doing and asked me to stop by a Tuesday group meeting he was leading of black men who were looking for help, hope, and opportunity. As I sat through the deeply emotional session with about twenty-five men, it was powerful to see how these men, through Christ and each other, were changing their lives. It was at this point I knew that John could transform others with his message of redemption, compassion, and forgiveness.

"*Bloodline* is a must-read for those interested in changing their own lives. It is a critical book for people working in the fields of social work, psychology, social justice, criminal justice, chemical dependency and violence prevention. *Bloodline* moves us from dealing with hypothetical and theoretical constructs of how to change the conditions of black men in America, to the nitty-gritty real-life experiences of black men on the streets of America. It offers a new direction and specific interventions that hold much promise for transforming our communities."

—GARY L. CUNNINGHAM, President & CEO,
Metropolitan Economic Development Association (MEDA)

"In order to understand what true transformation looks and feels like, you need to read the story of John Turnipseed's life. It is so compelling that this book should be required reading for all urban development workers, faith-based communities, and urban fathering and family program clients and centers. God's hand is so evident and present in John's story and his life. John's story is one in a million. By reading this book, you can both be a part of it and see how God can be at work in yours as well!"

—TIMOTHY CLARK, CEO, Urban Ventures

BLOODLINE

The True Story of
John Turnipseed
with Cecil Murphey

BroadStreet
P U B L I S H I N G

This is my story and the book is true and as accurate
as I can remember. In a few instances,
I have changed the names to protect their privacy.

BroadStreet Publishing Group, LLC
Racine, Wisconsin, USA
www.broadstreetpublishing.com

Bloodline: The True Story of John Turnipseed
With Cecil Murphey

© 2014 Five Stone Media

ISBN-13: 978-1-4245-4938-2 (print book)
ISBN-13: 978-1-4245-4951-1 (ebook)

Unless otherwise note, Scripture quotations are from the Holy Bible, New International Version®. NIV®. Copyright © 1973, 1978, 1984, 2011 by Biblica, Inc.™ Used by permission of Zondervan. All rights reserved worldwide. www.zondervan.com

Cover design by Scott Sample at www.initioadvertising.com
Interior design/typesetting by Katherine Lloyd at www.theDESKonline.com

Stock or custom editions of BroadStreet Publishing titles may be purchased in
bulk for educational, business, ministry, fundraising, or sales promotional use.
For information, please e-mail info@broadstreetpublishing.com

Printed in the United States of America

CONTENTS

FOREWORD

by Erwin Raphael McManus

I was given the great privilege to tell the story of John Turnipseed when Five Stone Media asked me to make a film based on his life. That request required me to not only know the story of John's life, but to know who the man really was—to see inside his soul. The story was intriguing to me as a filmmaker, but it also became deeply personal to me. Like everyone who meets John, I had become a part of his story. His life had touched my life.

On September 30, 2006, I was asked to speak on living a heroic life at a Heart of a Warrior men's event hosted by former military officer Greg Bourgond. The focus of the men's Advance centered around calling men to live lives of true honor and nobility. A group of businessmen who have since become my friends provided scholarships to several men from Urban Ventures, then led by Art Erickson.

Art is one of those rare individuals who lives his life in the service of others. Art carries a gravitas that comes only through living a life of courageous service to those whose lives are perilously close to self-destruction. There is always a tribe around Art that would never come together except by his hand. The rich and the poor follow Art and find each other. Art is in the business of second chances. He finds those who are one chance away from a new life. John Turnipseed was one of them.

I heard rumblings about John and his notorious past. To believe the stories, John played a key role in turning Minneapolis into "Murderapolis." Over thirty of his blood have served in prison. This was his family legacy. This is what he passed on to those who carried his name. This was his bloodline.

His namesake, known as Little Johnny, is still in prison to this day because he followed in his father's footsteps and later found himself an enemy of his father. John betrayed his son twice. The first time it cost him his son's future; the second it cost him his freedom. John made a choice that his son could not forgive. Little Johnny resented his father because his betrayal cost him his freedom, but his father knew that it saved his life and offered him a second chance.

It's a broken world when your best moment as a father is to surrender your son to the authorities to save his life. It was a strangely noble act in a worst-case scenario.

It was the beginning of the end for both of them. It was also a new beginning. Estranged for eleven years, they met for the first time at the men's Advance where I was speaking. Little Johnny was set to go to prison the day after the Advance ended. It was here that I glimpsed what the future would hold for John and his family. It was here that a different legacy began to overtake a history of violence.

John had become a different man. Not a perfect man; a new man. His rage replaced with an unexpected gentleness. A man once known for violence was now known for his compassion. All of John's bitterness was now replaced by forgiveness. His despair was overtaken by hope. His hatred replaced by love. His emptiness filled with faith.

Where once to follow John Turnipseed would lead you to prison, now it would lead you to freedom. If you asked John he would tell you it's all on account of Jesus. God became the Father that John never knew. Jesus gave John the peace for which his soul had always longed. His new brothers in faith gave him the family he always needed to walk this long hard road called life. It was Jesus who gave John his ultimate second chance. John chose to surrender his life to Jesus and it changed not only his destiny, but also his legacy.

All the blood John had shed in a life lived in darkness was now covered by the blood Jesus shed to bring him into the light. To bring this light into the world, to declare freedom to captives, to bring hope into a world filled with despair, this was now John's mission. Where once you could find John Turnipseed through a trail of blood, you can now find him through a trail of love. This is his legacy. This is his story. This is his bloodline.

Books are written in ink and on paper. Lives are lived out through blood, sweat, and tears. This is not a perfect story; it's a real one. It is a reminder of what God can create out of the rubble of our lives.

JT, it is an honor to be your brother, your friend, and to have had the privilege to tell your story. We are blood.

Let us fight the good fight until all mankind is free.

—ERWIN RAPHAEL MCMANUS
Author, lecturer, and pastor of Mosaic Church
in Los Angeles, California

1

BLOODLINE

I shouldn't be alive today.

A judge accurately called me a career criminal, which is a dangerous way of life and an easy way of death. Here are some of the reasons:

- Ten times, gangbangers have shot at me.
- Several times I was stabbed.
- Another time, I was thrown into the trunk of a car and my abductors took me out of the city to kill me.
- I was heavily into crack and cocaine and probably should have died of an overdose, especially after I began to mainline.
- For years, I was a pimp—which is an extremely unsafe profession.
- When I was in prison for ten years, another inmate tried to kill me.
- I was a thief. With a gun in my hand, I robbed countless homes and burglarized businesses.
- One time, when I broke into a home to steal their valuables, the husband fired a rifle at me at close range. But the shot missed me.
- I went on robbery sprees, and with a few other gang members, we often robbed five places in a single day.

And I felt no remorse.

I convinced myself that I had a right to take from people. My drugs made me feel invincible and I didn't care about going to jail. Several times I was institutionalized and jail or prison didn't bother me. Why should it? My best friends were incarcerated, so I had a good time with them. I always figured out ways to have sex with women and buy drugs or get anything I needed. Probably, lived better in jail than I did on the streets.

———⟋⟋⟍———

Some might say I became a career criminal because of a curse in our bloodline—and I wouldn't argue. The Bible speaks of God punishing evil people up to the third or fourth generation.* Even though Bible scholars reject the idea, a few people insist that all blacks are descendants of Ham, the third son of Noah, whom God cursed.

Curse or not, the bloodline of the Turnipseed family has been tainted, and I was the leader in the corruption. Not only was I a career criminal, but so are my sons, grandsons, nephews, and cousins. In four generations of Turnipseeds—all the same bloodline—most are or have been part of the corruption.

So it's easy to see why some have called us cursed. Even so, I'm determined to see this bloodline legacy stopped before I leave this life.

Perhaps one way to explain this is to talk about our family. In 1990, my son Little Johnny helped organize a family gang called Bloods, as in *blood relatives*. That name included everyone in the Turnipseed family as well as those who joined us through marriage such as the Fergusons and Edwardses. Many of the members wore a Boston Red Sox cap because it had a red B on it. To us the B stood for Bloods.

The leaders of the Bloods have always been members of my immediate family. I'm writing this at the age of fifty-nine, and the current gang considers me an elder statesman.

We changed the name of our gang to the Rolling 30s Blood Street Gang, although we still referred to ourselves as the Bloods. *Thirties* referred to the neighborhood between 30th and 39th Streets in South Minneapolis, which was under our control. And I mean complete control. No one committed crime there without our permission.

---

* See Exodus 20:5, Exodus 34:7, Numbers 14:18, and Deuteronomy 5:9.

I've been out of crime for twenty years, but even now I can make a call to help someone in need, and members of the gang will listen to me. I still make calls, but they no longer involve crime. These days, the calls are for the sake of peace or cooperation. I can do that because I'm a Turnipseed—an original Turnipseed—and in our community, an admired status still comes with that name.

That's not to brag—in fact, I'm ashamed—but I write this to show the widespread influence and power of the Turnipseed bloodline.

—⁓—

For the past twenty years, I've worked with dedicated individuals and organizations to redeem our family name and to destroy the memory of the Rolling 30s Blood Street Gang.

"How long do you think it will take for that to happen?" someone recently asked.

"Two generations," I answered. "The rising generation and their children. And I want to see that happen during my lifetime."

Family members in my generation have already received hundreds of years of prison time, been guilty of murder, prostitution, home invasion, armed robbery, theft, and drug dealing. And the Turnipseeds are more than a handful of people. In 2010, I went online and counted *thirty* members of our family who were incarcerated. That included two of my sons, four grandsons, uncles, nephews, and a number of cousins.

All Turnipseeds; all convicted criminals.

That's our bloodline.

But I've changed, and so can they, and together we can transform the Turnipseed bloodline and legacy.

My biggest regret is that I strayed from my childhood teaching. I went into a life of crime freely and intentionally. Only after I realized the emptiness of such an existence was I able to get help and make my life count. As long as God gives me breath, I will continue to work to remove the cursed influence of the Turnipseed bloodline.

—⁓—

My criminal career started when I was fourteen years old. And yet, if people looked at my beginnings, they wouldn't have expected me to turn into a criminal.

I was born in Selma, Alabama, September 14, 1954, and I'm the oldest surviving child in our family. Because two older boys died at birth, my mother, Earlene Turnipseed, referred to me as her miracle child. By the time I moved into a life of crime, I was the oldest of seven siblings, with six brothers—Isaiah, Sterling, Michael, Jerome, Darryl, Markalow, and one sister, Bonita.

Although my father, AB Turnipseed, wasn't affectionate, we were close during my early childhood. He took me everywhere with him. As a small kid, I worked alongside him picking cotton. I also helped him pick watermelons, pecans, and sugarcane (and I ate my share).

In some ways, we were an idyllic black family in the Deep South. We were a church-going family, and my father sang in the choir. That meant we were in church often. And the preacher was important to us—the most honored and respected man in our community. By the time I was five years old, I had begun to imitate him. On Sundays I wore a suit (which was later passed on to my younger siblings) and felt I looked like him.

"You're going to be a preacher, boy," my grandmother once said when she saw me imitate our pastor.

When I was seven years old, life changed—for all of us. My father went to Minneapolis, Minnesota, to get a job so he could provide a better life for us. After he returned, he took us to there to live. Not only was life different in the North, but we became a different family.

If there is a curse on our bloodline, that's when it began.

2

THE CURSE BEGINS

In less than two years from the time my father left Alabama, he became someone else. He was no longer the father I loved. Not only did he act in strange ways, he didn't even look like the father I knew. Instead of the natural kinky or nappy hair, he had straight, processed hair. He dressed in fashionable clothes. He even smelled different. He had stopped going to church, started drinking and cursing, and became violent—all things he had never done in Alabama.

Shortly after our arrival in South Minneapolis, this once-gentle man began to beat my mother—another thing he hadn't done before. Most nights I heard Mom crying and Dad cursing. He was drinking and mixing with rough men at work, which may have been a reason for the change. Or maybe the new city only gave him the opportunity to reveal who he really was all along.

While living in Alabama, Daddy never hugged me, but he had always been nice to me. But when he hit Mom, I felt it as if he were beating me. Because I was the oldest, I was supposed to take care of my mom and I couldn't. Even though I was still a kid, that sense of failure messed me up. No matter how I tried to protect her, it didn't stop him. The beatings continued for years.

As a result, I became like a father to my younger brothers, or at least I tried. Much of my criminal behavior formed around my trying to provide food, clothing, and toys for them.

For me, school was difficult in the North because I had a southern accent and the bullies picked on me. My bowl haircut, done by my mother, made bigger kids laugh. Besides that, I was small and skinny, and I had no big brothers to take care of me. On the playground, the bullies beat me up to make me talk so they could make fun of my way of speaking.

One time I said, "I'm going down the *screek* to get something to eat."

"What's a screek?" one tall kid asked before he laughed and punched me.

Another yelled at me, "It's *street*, you dummy!" (I never made that speech mistake again.)

The one good thing about being in Minneapolis was that Mom made me read and helped me understand the words. She also made sure I did my homework, and after my brothers entered school, I helped them. And in helping them, I also learned.

Dad, despite being mean and beating Mom, was hard working, and his boss at the Minneapolis Metal Coating Company on University Avenue promoted him to the job of supervisor. Once established in his new position, Dad persuaded my uncles, cousins, and many of his friends to come north. Most of them stayed at our house for a while and went to work with Dad.

Although the men made good money—as good as wages went for black men in those days—the job was still unsafe. Like slave labor, they worked twelve-hour shifts, six days a week. Metal coating was dangerous and injuries on the job were common. Some of the men developed cancer because of the acid in the air.

Even though Dad was a supervisor, he couldn't read or write. His name was AB Turnipseed—just two initials, which was common among the male Turnipseeds. Two of his brothers were my Uncle CL and Uncle AB. None of them was literate.

Since we were the first family of Turnipseeds in Minneapolis, that gave Dad special standing. Yet many of the relatives on my mother's side didn't like him. I often heard my aunties talk about him, and the things they said were horrible.

"You need to leave him, Earlene."

"He's no good for you," another auntie insisted.

"He's my husband," Mom answered to let them know she wouldn't leave him. And she never did. Despite the beatings (and some were real bad), she stayed with him and never looked at another man.

Although those first years in Minneapolis weren't the beginning of my life of crime, it was a dark period for me, and the seeds were planted. Every day seemed the same—horrible—and I dreaded getting up in the mornings. School was terrible. I couldn't tell anyone my dark home secrets, and I hated school so much I did mean things to get suspended.

One time, I put a tack in the teacher's chair, knowing that would force her to suspend me.

Another time, I lifted the hem of the teacher's dress and she slapped me. "You will end up in every prison in Minnesota!"

Although her words weren't completely accurate, she was right about my going to prison—more than once.

Because I became so disruptive at school, a psychiatrist examined me and classified me as having Attention Deficit Disorder. He prescribed Ritalin, which the school provided for free. I liked the drug because it made me high, even though it was supposed to be a downer for kids.

My schoolwork suffered because I didn't care. In that school, students received either an S for satisfactory or an N for not satisfactory. I received all S's in the beginning. But by my second year, most of my grades were N's.

I didn't have many friends, and even the few I had, I didn't invite to our house. I was too ashamed to let them see the rats and roaches.

While we lived in a cheap, infested apartment, Dad enjoyed the high life. He bought a new car and owned plenty of new clothes. Not only did he have a number of girlfriends, occasionally he brought them to our house. Other times, he spent the night with one of them. I liked it better when he went to their houses because it meant he wouldn't be home to beat up my mom.

Despite all the bad things Dad did, my mother never said anything against him. In time, that turned me against *her*.

I was twelve by the time all four of my younger brothers were in school, so Mom began working. She cleaned houses, which was about the only kind of work an uneducated African American woman could get. She also went to night school and earned her GED.

By then, I was making a little money shining shoes on the street corners, in the bus station, and in bars. Most of the time, however, I had to be home before Mom left for school because she put me in charge of my siblings with instructions to clean the house while she was gone.

About that time, I became friends with a kid I'll call Mose, who lived in the same apartment complex. We started hanging out together, and although he was my age, he was street smart. He had already figured out how to make a little money, and he agreed to cut me in on it.

He told me about a man who liked boys. Although I called it icky, later I realized it was a form of sexual molestation. When we went to the man's house, he gave us a Coke, a cookie, and either a quarter or a dollar so he could hold our penises while we peed. At first, I got only a quarter, but before long, like my friend, I also received a dollar.

We established a routine of going over there every Saturday afternoon. The man never did anything else to us, and I tried not to think about what he was doing. Instead, I focused on what I'd do with the money.

Usually after we each received our dollar, we hurried to the White Castle—the only fast-food hamburger place in our neighborhood. For a dollar, we could buy eight hamburgers. Occasionally, I saved a couple of my dollars so I could buy a sack of burgers and french fries and take them home to my brothers.

My life was miserable, and for a long time I didn't know any way to change it. Then my cousin Tommy Ferguson moved to Minneapolis, and my life of crime began.

3

A LIFE OF CRIME

When I was twelve years old, my older cousin Tommy Ferguson moved from Chicago to South Minneapolis. Although he had his own place, Tommy came around almost every day. Like my dad, he was a big man who also had processed hair. Immediately I was attracted to him because he was tough, nineteen years old, and nobody told him what to do.

What made me admire Tommy most was that he carried guns and knives. My dad was probably afraid of him because when Tommy was around, Dad didn't mess with Mom. That made me like Tommy even more.

Occasionally, Tommy stayed overnight. He was funny, and when he laughed, the sound filled the room. He liked me and we became close. Through his actions and kindness, Tommy replaced my dad. I promised myself that one day I would take care of my dad so he'd never beat Mom again; I would become the Tommy in our house.

"I'm going to teach you about life," Tommy said to me one day.

And I was eager to learn anything he wanted to show me.

As his first lesson, when I was still only twelve, he introduced me to his girlfriend. He let her give me my first sexual experience. That made me feel like a grown-up.

———

By the time Tommy became important to me, I had lost all respect for my mother and was mad at her for not standing up to Dad. My anger shifted to her for being passive and weak. "You let Dad beat you all the time," I yelled at her. "I don't like you!"

Another change was that after Tommy came into my life, I refused to take the Ritalin provided by my school. Grown men didn't need kids' drugs, and I wanted to do everything a grown man would do.

Tommy's next lesson was to get me a gun. He took me to a store on Lake Street, about four blocks from where we lived. He helped me select a .22 caliber pistol and paid for it. The transaction was illegal, of course, but I didn't care—in fact, it was exciting.

That was also the day I committed my first armed robbery. Together, Tommy and I robbed a barbershop outside our community. It was an intoxicating experience, although I almost threw up because of my nervousness.

During the robbery, I dropped my gun, then quickly picked it up, which caused Tommy to laugh as we hurried away. As scared as I was, I liked the rush. I felt like Thor, the god of thunder I had read about in one of my schoolbooks.

The next day, we robbed a small grocery store. That time, I felt no fear. The rush was so strong, I yelled and pushed people around, trying to please Tommy by my rough behavior.

Because I had successfully committed two robberies, I was a man! I couldn't wait to brag to my buddies.

Besides my first sexual encounter and armed robberies, Tommy introduced me to the folks at Hubert's Barbershop, where pimps and prostitutes hung out. Because I was Tommy's cousin, the hustlers paid me to run errands for them. I worshiped them and wanted to be like them. In my eyes, they were *real men*.

Now I had money; I didn't need anybody.

I had become a true criminal and was proud of myself. I committed several armed robberies on my own and won the approval of Tommy and his friends.

One day, when I was fourteen years old, I walked into the house and handed my mother a hundred-dollar bill. I was proud of myself and felt I was doing things for her that Dad never did.

Instead of thanking me, she stared at me as if I had put a snake into her hand. She started praying aloud, and then she yelled, "Get out! Something's wrong with you."

I don't know or care if she kept the money, but I had four more hundred-dollar bills in my pocket.

I was a man.

———

Although still fourteen, money and sex motivated me, and I couldn't get enough of either. Then a third motivator came into my life: street drugs. The men at Hubert's turned me on to acid, mescaline, and snorting cocaine.

Not only had I become a man among the grown-up men, I began to get respect from the kids at school. Word spread that I owned a gun, and after that, no student ever messed with me again. On the three or four blocks around our house, it seemed as if everybody now knew me, and the adults liked me. Even though I was robbing people, I never did anything bad in my own community.

Almost every day, I went outside our neighborhood, stole things, and came back. I gave most of the money to my brothers or to friends. Mom finally began to accept my money, although she didn't like it. Because Dad spent his money elsewhere, I bought the clothes and school supplies for my brothers. I'd buy anything for them and my friends. I wanted people to like me.

Everybody knew I was regularly expelled from school and that I was a Turnipseed. And because they knew I was tough, nobody messed with my brothers. In fact, they never had to fight the whole time they were in school because the other kids knew I would come after them if they hurt my family. I was earning respect, and that too was like a drug.

I hung out with three or four guys, who, like me, were involved in a delinquent lifestyle. I owned four guns, and I kept any weapons I found while burglarizing houses. By then, it felt normal to carry a pistol.

None of my friends owned guns. When I offered them one of mine, they refused. I laughed, saying they were afraid.

My criminal life had taken hold.

Although I robbed a lot of people, I didn't get caught.

For example, one day I walked into a gas station outside our area, shoved a gun in the cashier's face, and walked out with all the money in the register. That was quite a life, robbing grocery stores and gas stations—they were the easiest. And robbing them in the daytime was the quickest way to get the most money. I was in and out of a place in less than two minutes.

That year, I also learned to gamble. Without fail, I lost my money before the night was over. But I didn't mind: there were always people out waiting for me to rob them.

One day, I lost all my money at a gambling house. "I'll be right back," I said, and left. I didn't have a car, so I walked to Lake Street—which was busy—and robbed a place. (Sometimes I robbed the same store three or four times.) Within fifteen minutes, I returned with more money to gamble.

Did I know what I was doing was wrong? Of course, but I tried not to think about that. Drugs helped deaden my conscience. Another thing that may not make sense to some, is that robbing people was addictive—enticing, seductive. The adrenaline rushed through my body and I felt high while committing crimes, even when I wasn't using drugs.

When I walked into a place of business where I knew they had cash, and pulled out a gun, I felt like the biggest, baddest guy in the world. As a kid, I had watched old James Cagney films on TV and I saw myself as Cagney.

"Get back! Get back!" I'd yell. In my mind, I fantasized facing the police, who surrounded me. And like the movie star, I saw myself crying out, "Come on and get me, you dirty coppers."

I loved stealing. There was no bigger rush than leaving the house in the morning with no money and coming back that evening with a $1,000 in my pocket. I'd boast to my little brothers, "Look what I got." Then, as strange as it sounds, I'd say, "But you can't do what I do," because I didn't want to corrupt them.

I loved robbing people, even though my childhood church teachings said stealing was wrong. But by then, I was no longer going to church, and God didn't matter to me.

School didn't matter either. I stayed in school, but missed as often as I could. In those days, we had to go but it was a nuisance. I continued to be so disruptive in class that teachers barely tolerated me, and seemed glad when I didn't show up. I caught on to math easily, and, unlike many of my peers, I could read anything, so I passed the tests.

On days we had an exam, I came into the room, the teacher handed me the test, I wrote the answers, and left.

None of them ever objected. Yes, it was a good life for me.

4

GROWING IN CRIME

One day, Mose and I were walking down the street, and, as usual, I was carrying a gun. Mose didn't have one, but he was so strong he often bragged, "I don't need one." His method was to walk up behind someone, grab them, knock them down, take their money, and run. Like me, he'd never been caught.

We planned to meet another friend at a house owned by my cousin Terry, where we could have free sex with his prostitute.

"I don't have any money," Mose said and looked around.

"Come on, man, I'll give you some," I said. "Besides, Terry will let us have her free."

"Don't want no free sex." He shook his head. "And don't want *your* money. I want my own." He continued to look around, then pointed to an older woman. "I'm going to rob that lady there."

"You don't need to do that—"

"I want to."

"Okay," I said, realizing he was determined. "I'll wait."

It was the middle of the afternoon, and I walked on down to the corner where I stopped to watch him in action. He went up to the woman, pulled her off her feet, slammed her onto the ground, snatched her purse, and ran.

When Mose reached the corner, I joined him and we ran to Terry's house. Once inside, Mose opened the purse he had stolen. He found only fifty cents inside. He threw the purse across the room and started swearing and cussing the old woman for not having more money.

Just then, I looked out the window. Police officers were walking up and down the street. Assuming that it had to do with Mose robbing the old woman, I took the purse out back, set it on fire, and rushed back inside. A minute later, a police officer was in the backyard, stomping out the fire. He picked up the scorched purse and examined it.

I knew we were in trouble. So I picked up the phone, called my school counselor, and asked him to come and get me. He'd said he would pick me up any time I asked.

As soon as he arrived, I hurried outside and got into the car. Two police officers stared at me, but they didn't try to stop me.

I learned later that when Mose came out, they grabbed him.

The old woman died from his attack, and the police were determined to find her killer.

Mose confessed and implicated me; however, the police decided that I wasn't part of the robbery. At worst, I was an accessory after the fact. They didn't charge me.

But that murder messed up my mind and conscience. My friend killed her, but I was with him and saw him do it. Remembering that woman, more than forty years later, I'm still troubled.

Even though it had been a long time since I'd been in church, some of the teachings stayed with me. "Thou shalt not kill," echoed through my mind repeatedly. Our pastor preached that murder was the unpardonable sin. Because I had been with my friend and didn't stop him, therefore, I was as guilty before God as if I had killed her myself.

Many times I'd heard the preacher say, "If you take a life, you are doomed to hell."

No doubt about it. I was doomed.

———————

I didn't get sentenced for the death of the woman, but my time was coming. I continued committing burglaries, and kept getting away with them. My success made me careless.

Although I was a juvenile, I had easy access to all the drugs I wanted because I had become part of the underworld culture. Some of my friends, all older guys, provided the drugs because I had money.

My life had changed so much that every day I had to take drugs—to go to sleep, to wake up, to function during the day, to have sex, to not have sex—pretty much in order to do anything. Whenever I got ready to commit a robbery, I swallowed a combination of speed and downers so I wouldn't feel any emotions.

Once, while robbing a house, I was so high I took my eyes off the owner and instead focused on the cash. When I turned around, he was standing less than ten feet away, pointing a rifle at me. Just as he pulled the trigger, I ducked, and he missed.

When he fired, the rifle kicked and threw him off balance.

I snatched his gun and ran. I was shaking so bad I left the money, glad just to be out of the house and not lying dead on his floor.

Many years later, I told myself that God had kept that bullet from hitting me.

So all my robberies weren't successful; however, those home invasions were destructive in other people's lives.[*]

Tommy Ferguson moved on to other things. Instead of taking a new partner, I started doing the robberies by myself because I didn't want to share the money. There was so much money in what I was doing that all I needed was a big gun. The bigger the gun, the less resistance.

Parents didn't want their kids hanging with me. I think I even scared my own mom. But my little brothers idolized me because I protected them and gave them money and gifts. I made sure we had plenty of food and my brothers were never hungry. Now that they owned everything from tennis shoes to toys, they invited kids over to the house. People liked coming to our house to eat because I bought big packages of lunchmeat, cheese, crackers, candy, and Kool-Aid.

I kept telling myself I was living the good life—the best life—because I had everything. Yet I was miserable and depressed. Only by sniffing cocaine was I able to push away those emotions. For a time. They always came back.

---

[*] Home invasion refers to illegal and usually forceful entry to an occupied, private dwelling with intent to commit a violent crime, such as robbery, assault, rape, murder, or kidnapping.

My next step, even though I didn't know it, was to become a gang member.

Gangs were beginning to form in Minnesota, and one in particular tried to recruit me. My friend Warren Johnson, an older teen, wanted me to join his gang, the Four Corner Hustlers.

Their name meant they stationed one man in each of the four corners of an intersection. Each one controlled that corner and sold drugs. They were actually part of the Vice Lords criminal empire out of Chicago, and they wanted to establish themselves in Minneapolis. The Vice Lords, all African Americans, were the third largest gang in the world. And probably still are.

——————

Eartheil Wiley was a black nationalist, and I linked up with him and his group. He had convinced me that the police were evil and we should kill every one we could.

Eartheil had a powerful rifle, and he took my friend Kevin and me to his basement to teach us how to use it. He wanted me to shoot a cop on Fourth Avenue in our neighborhood. He got me so high I was willing to kill any cop.

We planned to go to a grassy, sloping terrace. Eartheil would call the police and say, "I just saw a black man carrying a gun break into a car. He's still there." When the police car arrived, we would shoot the officers.

While we were driving to the place, Eartheil told me, "You're going to be the shooter."

"I can't," I said, "I'm nearsighted." That was true, although I refused to wear glasses.

We began arguing and Kevin said he didn't want to shoot the cops either.

All three of us were in Eartheil's car, and he was yelling and driving so fast, he ran into a car. Eartheil grabbed the rifle, hopped out of the car, and took off running.

Kevin and I were right behind him, but as we passed the car we heard the driver moaning. If it had been a gangbanger situation, I wouldn't have cared. But the driver was a woman, what we called a civilian, so I went back. She'd had nothing to do with the crime, but since she was hurt, I felt it was wrong to leave her.

When I got closer, I realized the woman was pregnant. The police showed up and took her to the hospital. I later learned that she almost lost the baby. However, because I came back, they arrested me.

"Hey, I was just walking along and saw the accident," I claimed. "I get arrested because I stopped to help her? That's not right."

I went to jail and was put on probation.

Eartheil was well-known by the police for being ruthless, but he had an almost hypnotic influence on several of us. That summer, he convinced us to throw Molotov cocktails at an apartment building with old, white people inside, hoping it would burn down. That's how crazy we were. And we didn't care. We only wanted to get rid of every white person in our neighborhood.

Many of those elderly people were hurt in the fire, and went to the hospital. But at least no one died.

———

In 1971, at age seventeen, I was so depressed and miserable over my life, I smoked a lot of dope and took enough pills to purposely kill myself.

I waited to die. Instead, I vomited up the pills. Someone in my family found me, in a catatonic state, and took me to the hospital.

That didn't stop my criminal activity. I did more robberies and hurt a lot of people.

One memory especially troubled me. We occasionally went into an all-white gang's neighborhood. If they caught us in their territory, they beat us up. One night, I went over there while my friends hid nearby. I taunted a white kid. He took off after me. I made him chase me over the bridge where my friends were waiting. They grabbed him, beat him, and hit him in the head with a pipe wrench. He didn't die, but perhaps he should have. He was so badly hurt, he suffered from brain damage and serious physical problems.

The picture of that teenage white boy struggling while five of us black teens repeatedly hit him, haunted me for a long time.

I actually enjoyed the violence, but every once in a while it would catch up to me. Most of all, I enjoyed the power it gave me. I was recognized as the "beast on the block." I also learned that if I was violent enough, I could take anything I wanted and no one would bother me.

5

PREPARING FOR BIGGER THINGS

Because of the death of the old woman, Warren invited me to become an honorary member of his gang. I shrugged, trying to appear indifferent.

"Not anyone can join us," he said, "and you gotta meet the requirements to become one of us."

"Yeah? What are those?"

"Two things. You gotta have a gun—"

"I got four of them."

Warren smiled before he added, "And you gotta have an *association* with murder." He didn't say I had to have killed—which I hadn't—but being with Mose when that woman died, qualified me.

"Got that too," I said with pride.

"Then you can join us."

"And I get to lead a gang?" I asked.

Warren shook his head. "Nah. Maybe later, but we gotta know you a little better."

"You already know me," I said. "Besides, I don't want someone telling me what to do."

We talked for perhaps twenty minutes before I walked away from him. His coming to me made me decide to start my own gang, where I would be in charge. And that's exactly what I did. Within a couple of days, I had my little gang. The first member was my friend Kevin, who was Warren's brother.

Even though he tried to recruit me, Warren hadn't killed anyone or even been implicated in murder. Shortly after that, however, he robbed and killed a cab driver. He was caught, convicted, and served a long prison term.

Two men Warren had recruited made their mark by killing. One of whom murdered a newspaper reporter, was caught and sentenced.

The other, seventeen-year-old Ricky, was very impressionable. A gang member handed him a gun, and pointed to a man walking down the street. "Shoot and kill him." Ricky did as he was told. He was also caught and convicted.

Other gang leaders tried to recruit me, probably because of my criminal element. One man who wasn't even part of a gang wanted me to partner with him. He looked like me, and people often thought we were blood brothers. I didn't like that because he was sadistic and into cruel robberies. He beat his victims for no reason. But I didn't do anything like that.

"No, I'm a loner," I said, "and I don't work with anyone."

———⟡———

One day, I loaned my car to a man we called Fast, who was my cousin Betty's boyfriend. He drove downtown, parked, and walked into a jewelry store just off Main Street in downtown Minneapolis. Without saying a word, he robbed the place, and shot and killed the man who worked there. Then Fast came back to South Minneapolis and returned my car.

An hour later, I was driving around when police cars from all directions converged on me. I didn't understand why.

"Out of the car," one of the officers ordered.

A second policeman stared at me, shook his head, and said, "He's not the one."

"I don't know what you're talking about," I said.

"Your car was definitely identified in a murder, and it's the same license number," the first officer said. "Who was driving your car earlier today?"

"Just my cousin Betty," I said. "Go ask her." I didn't know Fast's real name, besides, one of the unspoken rules in our criminal culture was not to snitch on anyone.

The cops went to Betty's house and found Fast there. He still had the murder weapon on him.

Those were the type of people I was hanging with—individuals who would kill and it meant nothing to them. I fit right in with that crowd because other than murder, crime didn't bother me. At least not outwardly. I had learned to compartmentalize my emotions. And it worked. Most of the time.

——

On another occasion, I was riding in a car with three friends, all of us drunk, and we had guns in the trunk of the car. The driver hit a pregnant woman. She was badly hurt and almost lost her baby.

The police got involved, but I wasn't driving, so I didn't get charged. And they didn't search the trunk or we would have been in more trouble.

The police caught me in the act several times. The first time was for burglarizing a house and putting a gun to the heads of the people while I robbed them. Another time, a police officer nabbed me while I was trying to rob a grocery store. I went to court for both of those crimes.

A few things about me differed from the other thugs I hung with. I knew how to act, put on a smile, and I could speak good English. I didn't have tattoos or wear excessive jewelry, and I didn't have processed hair. Most folks in the neighborhood considered me a good kid who lived down the street.

Because I was different, most judges liked me. One even called me "a pleasant young man."

That didn't keep me out of jail, but it brought me lighter sentences.

Twice, I was sent to Glen Lake County Home. The first time was in 1969. I was there for nine months.

I didn't mind going to Glen Lake because my girlfriend snuck in pills whenever she visited. Mostly she brought in "sofers"— zombie pills. I never felt anything after taking them. Other times, she brought a mixture of red devils (a downer) and black dexes (an upper). We called them speedballs. The combination made me high and kept me from sleeping. They also made me think I could drink as much alcohol as I wanted and not be affected. During most of my nine months in Glen Lake I was high on some type of drug—white crosses, red devils, black dexes, wine weed, acid, Dexedrine, Valium, or sofers. And when I got out, I found out that having been locked up made me even more of a hero in the eyes of my friends.

———

At Glen Lake, they had guided group interaction, a therapeutic thing that came out of New York State. The leaders told us it encouraged positive peer culture, and taught kids how to interact in groups and heal themselves.

Whatever was supposed to happen to me, didn't. The administrator labeled me a psychopath. But I also was very much a leader—and it would show up even more when I was an adult in prison.

When I went to those positive peer culture groups, I twisted everything anyone said, and took over as the leader. They switched me to another peer group, it didn't matter because I took over that one as well. I didn't use strong-arm tactics. The kids just trusted me (or were afraid to go against me). If trust or fear didn't work, I'd meet with the kids individually in their rooms and talk with them. That tactic never failed.

I don't know how I influenced those other kids—I suppose it's a gift that I can't explain—and I was able to do it without violence.

Some of my friends were tougher and meaner than I was, but they relied strictly on their physical strength. I was a stronger leader who knew how to make things happen, and so they worked for me. For instance, I figured out how we could sneak out of our cabin at night, go to the girls' cottage, have sex, and we never got caught.

The only way anyone could "graduate" from Glen Lake and go home was if the kids voted for a person to leave. When I decided I'd had enough, I asked my peers to vote. They didn't dare not vote for me.

———

Within days of being on the streets again, I went out-of-control crazy. I got into robbery, drugs, women, and fighting other gangs who wanted to operate in Turnipseed territory.

Yolanda, one of my female cousins, got into an argument with a woman down the street from where we lived. Yolanda came to me and complained about her. That wasn't unusual. Family regularly called on me to settle disputes, even though I was still a teenager. Everyone in the community knew I carried a gun, which intimated them. They considered me one of the tough guys. I liked being able to take care of family.

"I'll go with you," I said to my cousin. "She won't trouble you again."

I swaggered behind my cousin as we headed down the street. The woman who had argued with Yolanda was scrubbing her porch. She invited us to join her inside. Just as we reached her door, the woman threw the cleaning liquid in our faces.

With eyes stinging and temporarily blinded, my cousin and I raced down the block, trying to wipe the stuff off our faces.

When we reached our house, one of my aunties was there.

"A woman threw something on me and I can't see," I said.

"It was probably lye. Boy, get me some milk. That will dilute it."

We all went to the kitchen. I pulled out a carton of milk from the refrigerator and handed it to her. Because it wasn't a strong mixture, we were lucky and had no aftereffects.

As my aunt was washing our eyes with the milk, Tommy Ferguson walked in. "What happened?"

After I told him, I said," I'm going back down there and take care of that woman."

"I'll take care of her." He headed toward the door.

"Wait a minute. I'll be right with you."

Tommy waved me back. "I got this."

"No, I'll go with you."

"I got this!" His firm tone of voice told me he wanted to take care of it by himself.

As soon as my eyes were all right, I ran out of the house and raced toward where the woman had thrown lye on me. Before I got there, I heard a gunshot. I ran faster.

When I got there, Tommy was lying on the ground with blood all over him. He was dead by the time I reached him.

Later, I found out that just as the wife had done to us, the husband had invited him inside. The man opened the door, grabbed a shotgun and fired, hitting Tommy in the chest.

I was so upset I don't remember everything that happened, but someone called the police and they arrested the woman's husband for discharging a firearm within the city limits. He received a one-year sentence.

I couldn't understand why that was the only charge against him. But Tommy was a ruffian, a thug, well-known by the police, and I guessed they were glad to get rid of him.

A few weeks later, somebody burned down that house. The woman and her children moved from the community they'd lived in for years. That was a good thing because none of us Turnipseeds was going to let Tommy's killer come back.

I grieved over the loss of Tommy, my father figure. Justice had not been done. And my anger grew.

6

FOLLOWING CRIMINAL FOOTSTEPS

The second time a judge sentenced me to Glen Lake County Home it was for armed robbery. Almost as soon as I was inside, a woman on the staff made fun of my name. That remark enraged me. They didn't know I was high, but it intensified my anger.

Even though she was nine months pregnant, I pushed her against the wall, and grabbed a woodcutting tool. A male staff member grabbed my arm before I could hurt her. If he hadn't stopped me, I would have killed her.

In that short time I was so disruptive, the superintendent called the judge, "I don't care what you do with him," he said, "but I don't want him in our institution."

They let me go and I assume they suspended the sentence. I'd only been inside about forty-five minutes.

The next step in following the criminal life was being sentenced for one year to Red Wing State Reform School for Boys. If I hadn't messed up in school, I probably wouldn't have been sentenced.

In those days, junior high teachers passed anyone who showed up for classes. Since I could read well and was good at math, I enrolled in high school. But that lasted only one week because I threatened the principal.

Not only was I suspended from that school, I was not allowed to enroll in any other public school in Minneapolis or Hennepin County.

"Hey, this is great," I told my friends. That boast made me seem like an even bigger man. And it earned me more respect from the older gang members. Without school, I was living "the good life," with all the money, drugs, and sex I wanted.

Because I wasn't yet sixteen years old, I couldn't drop out. So I was placed in Red Wing. It was one of the first alternative schools in Minnesota, but other guys told me that regardless of which state, reform schools were all the same. Ours was filled with mostly African Americans, although a white kid came in every once in a while.

I stayed out all night partying and stealing, even though I had to be at school by eight thirty every morning. Sleeping through class was all I remember doing, which is what most of the others did. When we weren't sleeping, we smoked or partied right there in the classroom. No one taught us anything.

Whenever white folks—inspectors of the system—came to visit, our teacher would awaken us, make sure we had books in front of us, and give the visitors a tour of the place. As soon as they left, we went back to whatever we had been doing.

———

Despite my own behavior, I insisted my brothers keep up their attendance in the public schools. If I caught them playing hooky, I'd beat them up. I believed it was important for them to have an education so they'd never end up in jail.

I was more than forty years old before I understood my real motivation toward my siblings. Subconsciously, I tried to be the father to them I never had. I made sure none of the gangbangers allowed them to become involved in criminal activities with them. Unlike my father, I wanted to protect my siblings.

Unfortunately, my plan didn't work. All of my brothers ended up becoming drug addicts or alcoholics. But only two brothers went to prison, so maybe I made some difference in their lives.

During my wild, teenage years, all of my friends were older—the shady characters in the neighborhood that my cousin Tommy Ferguson introduced me to. All of them had been in and out of reform school and prison. Because they liked me, they looked out for me. Without them, I would have been in even bigger messes.

I developed a foul mouth. If anyone argued with me, I turned disrespectful and violent. People nicknamed me Taz, for Tasmanian Devil, because of my temper.

The next time I was caught robbing someone, a judge sentenced me to one year at the State Training School in Red Wing, Minnesota, a place for tough juveniles. I was fifteen years old. And like many of the hoodlums in my community before me, I had taken the next step toward adult prison.

Red Wing was an hour's drive from South Minneapolis, surrounded by bluffs. It looked like a college campus, but it had lock-up cottages. One cottage was fenced in like a penitentiary. That's where they put the kids who tried to escape.

I wasn't considered one of those in danger of taking off. So along with five other tough and fast kids, I was allowed to be a "flag." The six of us wore green sashes. Whenever any kids ran away from the reform school, an alarm sounded and we could go after them.

Because the school was on a bluff, we could see the kids tracking across the fields below. We flags pursued them through the fields, along roads, or up the steep bluffs. We kept running until we caught them—and we did every time. They always gave out before we did.

After we caught them, we beat them up before dragging them back to Red Wing. For "our good deed" we were rewarded with snacks and extra food, got to see movies, and were allowed to stay up later than other kids.

In reality, we were a legally sanctioned gang of thugs. We justified our behavior by saying we had to be tough so the other kids wouldn't retaliate.

"If you try to run," I pointed out, "that's a sign of disrespect toward us. We don't like being disrespected." As crazy as that might sound, they got the message. No kid ever ran away a second time.

When I entered Red Wing, I received the number 28842. It was a prison number. We received it early because the authorities figured it was only a matter of time until we were convicted and locked up as adults.

The people in charge at Red Wing couldn't make me do anything I didn't want to do. For instance, I refused to go to the classes they provided, and I proved my toughness by not being afraid of any kind of punishment. As a result, I spent a lot of time in isolated lockup—essentially solitary confinement.

Only one person could make me act right. His name was Father Capoochi. He was short and broad-shouldered, with black hair and piercing eyes. He reminded me of James Cagney. Whenever Father Capoochi came to the facility, I stopped cursing and fighting. I deeply respected him, wanted his approval, and didn't want him to be mad at me.

But he never got angry with me, even when he learned about the bad things I'd done. Although when I disappointed him, that made me feel worse than if he'd been furious.

"Johnny, why are you doing this?" he asked time after time in that calm, loving voice of his.

I usually shrugged, dropped my head, and mumbled, "I don't know."

"I want you to go back to class."

"Okay." I never argued.

"And I want you to behave."

"Yes, Father." And I did—for a few days.

The priest could get me to do anything because I knew he loved me. He didn't say those words, but when I was with him, I knew he cared and wanted the best for me. I loved that man so much, sometimes I acted up just so he would have to come and stop my bad behavior.

Father Capoochi always showed up when he was called, even in the middle of the night. (I tested him on that.) Often he had to visit me in a "strip cell." There was nothing in the room, not even a toilet or a chair. My feet were handcuffed to the ground, my arms spread out and handcuffed to a window covered with a wire-mesh screen. And I was naked.

Sometimes there would be as many as eight of us locked in one strip cell. During the summer, guards threw water on us and opened the windows so the mosquitoes would come in and bite us.

Whenever Father Capoochi found out I'd been put in a strip cell, he showed up within minutes and got the guard to release me.

The last time he came, I told him I didn't like the teachers and I wouldn't go to school. He didn't argue or try to convince me to go back. But the discouraged look on his face was enough to get me to return.

One time, I caught a bad cold while in isolation at Red Wing. A guard escorted me to the doctor's office, still in handcuffs. On the way, I saw an older, muscular staff member, Mr. Drews, who was weight-lifting 260 pounds.

I stopped, ignoring the guard's prodding. "Wait a minute, dude." I watched as Mr. Drews counted to fifty.

"Hey!" I yelled.

Mr. Drews turned his head, glanced at me and looked away.

"Hey, I'm talking to you, man."

He ignored me. And the guard forced me to keep moving.

On my way back from the doctor's office, Mr. Drews was still there, doing some fancy lifting with two huge dumbbells. Pretty impressive for a big, old white dude.

"Man, how do you do that?" I asked, wanting to know how to develop muscles like his.

He stared at me. "You're a dummy. And I don't talk to dummies." Without another word he went back to his exercise.

After I was released from isolation, I went to see Mr. Drews. In my most respectful voice, I asked, "Will you teach me how to lift weights like you do?"

"Nope. Not unless you go to school."

"But I hate school."

"If you're ever going to get any kind of decent job on the outside, you need a GED. If you want, I can help you study for it."

"I don't need to study."

"Yeah, you do. It's a tough test. Some of our boys have had to take it four or five times."

He was adamant about my studying, so I tricked him. Unknown to Mr. Drews, I picked up a book from the library about studying for the GED. A month later, I signed up to take it. To my surprise, Mr. Drews was the one who administered the test. I was sure he expected me to fail because I'd been so cocky and refused to study.

The next day, he told me I had passed my GED. I knew he was proud of me—not that he said the words, but I could tell.

"And I passed it the first time without studying." (I lied because I was proud of being able to pass by studying on my own.) "So now you can teach me to lift weights."

"Yep, you did your part. So I'll do mine."

As Mr. Drews worked with me in weight training, I learned that he was a teacher and the state weight-lifting champion in Minnesota.

He pushed me hard. "Come on, John, get it up. Do it!" Whenever I added another ten pounds, he patted me on the back and gave me this big old hug.

Within a short time, he'd trained me. Then he took me to a weight-lifting conference. I was pretty strong for my size and competed in one category. I took fifth out of about twenty-five men. Those guys were professional weight lifters, and I was only a kid and an amateur.

One of the conditions of Mr. Drews training me was that, even though I had gotten my GED, I still had to go to school, and not cause problems. I went to the classes, and although I didn't learn much, I stayed out of trouble. I stopped fighting the staff and the other kids because I really wanted to be around this dude. It was fun. Besides Father Capoochi, Mr. Drews became the only positive influence in my life.

I never would have been a teacher later, if he hadn't convinced me to go back to school.

Shortly before my sixteenth birthday, I went before an adult parole board, hoping they would release me. I did my best to look and sound like a nice down-the-street kid who had just made a mistake. I spoke politely and appeared contrite. They paroled me.

Of course, I kept coming back. And each time I returned, my friends welcomed me as a hero. I was tough. And I knew how to beat the system.

7

FATHER FIGURES AND FATHERHOOD

Father Capoochi was the first positive father figure for me. Art Erickson would become the second, even though I tried to ignore him for years.

I'm not sure when Art entered my life, but it was around 1970, about the time Tommy Ferguson died. He was the youth minister at Park Avenue United Methodist Church. Art lived in our African American community (and still does). Through his church, he ran a program that had the best outdoor basketball courts in the area.

Art was a couple of inches shorter than I am, and I'm five ten. Even then, his piercing blue eyes seemed to look right into my soul, which made me uncomfortable. Art spoke with a seriousness in his voice that pushed me to reflect on my life choices. I didn't like thinking about the way I was living, so it was easier to ignore him.

I wanted nothing to do with him because he represented change—and I wasn't willing to be reformed. I was a thug with the power to intimidate people. My friends and fellow gang members would have laid down their lives for me, and I would have done the same for them. And that was the kind of life I wanted.

But Art wouldn't give up. He wanted me—and all my friends—to go to school, and especially to church to learn more about God. But right then, God was not what I wanted.

At Park Avenue, Art was in charge of a food shelf where needy families came for free groceries. He was obviously interested in our neighborhood and arranged trips and events for teens like me, but I was too tough to get involved.

Art seemed to be almost everywhere I went, showing up like the so-called bad penny. I'd go to watch my little brothers play basketball and he was there. That was all right, but he kept trying to talk to me about God. Most of the time, I ignored him. At other times, I made jokes, laughed at him, and told him I had better things to do. No matter what I said or did, that man didn't give up on me.

Everyone in the community respected him. Once, he caught me shooting dice with friends, and he encouraged them to stop. "Ignore him," I said. "Let's keep playing." But they quit. After the other guys ran off, I, being the tough one of the group, stayed to face him. Sometimes I yelled at Art; most times I just ignored him.

But Art didn't give up on me. Not then. Not later. Not ever.

"I know what you're selling and I'm not buying the Jesus thing."

Art just smiled. No matter what I said, he didn't take offense. He never got angry or scared, and was always upbeat. Art never used church talk with me—which I liked—and he always had funny comebacks.

One time, I told him to go to hell.

"Too hot for me," he said and laughed.

Doesn't that man ever give up?

Even though I didn't know it, the day would come when Art would be a powerful force in the new direction for my life.

———

At age sixteen, and a few weeks after my release from Red Wing, I learned that Sheron, my seventeen-year-old girlfriend, was pregnant with my child. She'd been a virgin when we met and conceived during one of her visits to me at Red Wing.

I was upset when she told me because I didn't want to be a father. I cursed myself for being careless and having sex without a condom. But I wanted to do the right thing and stand by her. She was my first love and my sister's best friend. She was pretty, dressed like a tomboy, and fought like a boy. And I really liked her.

A few weeks after my release, I beat up a friend because I was high. And when I was high, I acted a little crazy.

Then I went to visit Sheron in her basement apartment. She was in her last month of pregnancy, and seemed happy to see me. I sat down next to her and we talked about the baby.

Suddenly, she screamed, "Willie!"

I turned around and saw her sister's boyfriend. He hated me because he felt I had something to do with his cousin's death (which I didn't). We began to argue and Willie pulled out a gun.

Before I could react, Willie fired three times. One of the bullets struck my arm. The basement had only one way out, and I knew if I didn't do something, he'd shoot me again. So I jumped up and ran straight toward him. Willie dropped the gun, raced out of the room, and up the stairs.

Sheron started moaning. I turned and found her lying on her back on the floor. Blood was everywhere. As I looked more closely, I saw a hole on the left side of her belly and another on the right side.

I called an ambulance. The ride to the hospital seemed endless. As I stared at her face, I wanted to pray for her, but I didn't know how. "Hold on, hold on," I said over and over.

Even though Willie shot me, it didn't hurt much because it hadn't shattered any bones. I watched, while a doctor in the ER pulled out the bullet and stitched up my arm. As soon as he finished, I went to check on Sheron.

It was a miracle that the fetus hadn't been hit. That night at the hospital, my baby, Lisa, was born by caesarian. Despite the way I felt before, when I saw her, my heart melted and I fell in love with my first child.

Since I was feeling fine, I left. But Sheron and Lisa stayed in the hospital a few days.

———

I wanted to give Lisa all the love I had never received, but I didn't know how. I'd helped bring her into this world and I wanted to protect and love her. "I'm a father now," I said to myself.

But at age sixteen, I didn't know what being a father meant. I certainly had no role model to follow. By then, I hated Dad and no matter what I did, I didn't want to be like him.

Like other irresponsible young males, I never married the mother of my child, and she was soon out of my life. Eventually, Mom stepped in and raised Lisa.

Without realizing it, however, I was soon following the pattern I had seen in our home. I became short-tempered, ill-mannered, and, also like my father, disrespectful of women, including Sheron. As I said to one of my street friends, "When all else fails, violence works."

Despite my vicious tendencies, one of my teachers, Mrs. Anders, must have seen something good still left, and refused to give up on me. Long after I left her school, she wrote to me regularly. She even kept track of me through social media. Forty years later, to my surprise, Mrs. Anders sent me some of my assignments, which she'd kept. Although, had I stopped to think about it, keeping and treasuring her letters made me quite a contradiction.

Perhaps just as strange, I knew I was living contrary to everything my mother and my childhood pastor had taught me. No one had to tell me it was wrong to hurt or rob people. I wasn't born to do those awful things. In my heart, I was guilty as charged—in fact, I felt more guilt inside than anything the lawyers and judges said against me. But whenever a little voice inside tormented me, I shut it off. Most of the time.

Hanging with men who were as evil as I was helped quiet the "good voice." But when I was alone, guilt and self-hatred stirred in me so bad I knew only one way to override my conscience: drugs and more drugs.

I quit school and avoided contact with any decent person I knew. Art Erickson, however, still popped into my life on a regular basis. Each time I saw him, I felt guilty. So I avoided him as much as possible.

I thought of myself as a king—a ruler over other thugs I could control and make all the decisions for. The guys who weren't as smart as I was became part of my gang. Maybe that was intentional, I don't know, but I could figure out things and plan. Without guidance, most of them could think of only their immediate pleasure and violence. So they listened to me.

The one thing I can say in my own defense—which isn't much—I never led younger kids into crime. I kept robbing people, but either alone or with older guys.

8

TEACHING DAD A LESSON

In 1973, while I was on probation from Red Wing, I was supposed to find a job and become a worthwhile member of society. I tried a few places, but nobody wanted to hire me. No big surprise.

My mother finally asked Dad to give me a job, even though I didn't want to go to work for anyone, especially him. We were hardly speaking to each other during that time. But he found a job for me where he worked.

The first morning at 5:00, he pulled up in front of the house where Sheron and I lived. I got inside the car and didn't say anything for a few minutes. I hated my dad and was working up the courage to confront him.

When he stopped at the plant, I put my hand in my pocket and wrapped my fingers around my .38 caliber pistol. "If you ever hit my mother again," I said slowly and in a low voice, "I'll blow your brains out."

"What?" His dazed look made me realize that he had not expected anything like that.

"You heard me."

Dad cursed and reached for his gun. I was quicker. I pulled mine out and shoved it in his face, the way I did when I robbed people.

I stared at his smaller gun, a .22, and looked into his eyes, hoping he could see the hatred I felt for him.

For a few seconds, Dad stared back. Then he flinched. "Okay." He put his gun down. "Now, get out of my car."

I smiled. Why not? I had won.

I got out of his car slowly, wanting to let him know I wasn't afraid of him, even though I was. "Don't forget what I said." I walked away without looking back at him or the factory.

I was proud of myself. I didn't need my father, and now he knew how much I detested him.

Then why did I feel so bad?

I hurried out for a drug fix.

———

After my threat, Dad never hit my mother again. But they were still married, and he came to see her from time to time. He impregnated her on one of his visits, and Mom finally had a baby girl, whom she named Bonita. Mom had always wanted a daughter. Now that she had one, she made it clear to Dad that she didn't want any more children.

Even though I was angry at Mom for letting Dad impregnate her again, I also admired her because she never spoke against him.

Shortly after that, Dad divorced Mom and married another woman. He tried that beat-her-up thing and she didn't go for it. I don't know details, except that one time when he started beating her, she grabbed a pistol and shot him in the head. He didn't die. But I'm pretty sure he never hit her again.

I didn't care that he'd been shot. I wouldn't have been sorry if she had killed him, or so I told myself. At least he'd be out of my life forever.

Except he wasn't. I may have hated him, but, like any kid, I yearned for his love. Although there was no affection and no relationship between us, and never would be, even today I carry that "father hole" inside me.*

———

Everyone in the community seemed to know who I was. Many of the court-appointed counselors tried to reach me, and they were honest in their intent. Their hearts were in the right place. Problem was, I didn't want to change.

---

* Twenty years later, I turned that pain into healing by teaching men how to be fathers and helping them reconcile with their children.

Why should I? I ran my own gang, although we didn't call it that. Organized gangs were a Chicago thing, my cousin Tommy had told me. We didn't have an official name or identity. They were just "my boys" and I took care of them.

My life of crime continued and I became even more powerful in the neighborhood. Twice, I was stabbed in fights with other guys. Some of my boys got angry and they responded by doing a lot of cutting and stabbing. But using a knife wasn't my way to get even. I took care of my enemies by shooting them—intentionally not killing them. Though I wouldn't have admitted it, I didn't want anyone to die at my hand. But by being shot, they got the message.

My reputation became solid in the community. But I still felt guilty and hated myself and my life. I dealt with my guilt by getting drunk more often or increasing the amount of drugs I needed to get high. Alcohol and drugs made me feel like a different person. I thought of myself as Batman.

Except I wasn't a comic-book hero. And when I came down from the high, I felt worse than before.

———

One day when I was really high, I met with my friend Nat. He'd never been arrested or gotten in any serious trouble. I got him so high that he was ready for anything. As we talked, one of us mentioned a drug dealer in our area who always kept large amounts of cash and drugs in his home. Nat decided it was a good idea for us to rob the man.

We took a mixture of drugs, which made us feel invincible. "We're going to do this!" he shouted. He was so high he had no fears or thoughts of failing.

At three o'clock in the morning, we went to the drug dealer's house. The weather was terrible—heavy rain with thunder and lightning. We kicked in the door. That's how crazy we were. But instead of the drug dealer, we found a middle-aged woman inside. We had received bad information and were at the wrong house.

"Watch her," I told my friend, "while I look through the house." No point in walking away from a perfectly good robbery opportunity.

I had just gone into the next room when the woman screamed. I raced back. The woman lay on the floor, moaning. Nat had hit her with a club. Later we learned he broke her hip.

"Don't do that again," I said, unable to look at her. "Go upstairs and see what you can find to steal." I glared at him and he knew I meant business.

"Okay," Nat said, then took off.

I remembered as a child, hearing my mother writhing in pain after one of my dad's beatings. But we were there to rob this woman. I wasn't supposed to feel compassion. That was a sign of weakness.

Still, her crying touched me. She looked up at me with fear in her eyes. I forgot about being strong and that I was a robber. I whispered comforting words while I tried to figure out what to do.

Nat came back downstairs, cursing and grumbling that he hadn't found much of value. If I hadn't been kneeling next to the woman, I think he would have hit her again.

"I'm hungry." He went into the kitchen and turned on the light.

Before he had finished eating, a loud banging on the door interrupted us. "Police!" a deep voice said.

I discovered later that while Nat was taking food from the refrigerator, the next-door neighbor awakened and looked out her window. When she saw a black man in the house, she called the police.

Nat and I were arrested and charged with home invasion. It was my first adult crime.

The woman told the police that my friend had hit her but I stopped him and tried to help her. Nat served a year in a workhouse in Minneapolis, where he worked inside the jail to finish his sentence.

My sentence was one year of work release in the same facility. That meant I could go home on the weekends. I could also leave the premises every day to go to work but had to return at night. Since I didn't have a job, a friend claimed that I worked for him.

The workhouse charged rent, and as I remember, it was twenty dollars a day. To my way of thinking, the police were forcing me back into crime so I could pay my rent.

During my year of work release, I stole and robbed—though not as heavily as before. This experience further elevated me as a tough guy to the gangbangers in our neighborhood. But inside, I was scared. If I got caught while on work release I would receive a severe sentence.

I couldn't carry a pistol, so I had to do what I called the sneak-thief way. Maybe I secretly wanted to get caught—I don't know. I do know I became careless. I started sleeping all day and slacked off on robbing people, and before long I'd used up everything I'd stolen.

"I'm going to somebody's house and get me some money!" I vowed to myself.

One afternoon, I was walking through an area that wasn't part of my territory—high on drugs, as usual. I spotted a woman in a back-yard. I knew it would be easy. But I only had a knife on me. And knives can be dangerous because it's easy to accidentally hurt someone or be hurt in the process. Unlike some of my criminal friends, I didn't enjoy hurting people.

I went inside the house, found a nice sum of money, and smiled. As I walked outside, a patrol car pulled up. Police officers invited me to get into the vehicle.

Since no one had been in the house, I couldn't be charged with home invasion. My only crime was theft.

Later, I discovered that a neighbor saw me entering the house and called the police.

When I went to court, my judge was the same one who'd sentenced me to the workhouse. He stared at me and shook his head. "What are you doing here? You're supposed to be at work."

I didn't care what happened to me. My life was miserable and I hated everything about it.

"You are hereby sentenced to ten years at the St. Cloud State Reformatory."

The reformatory was actually a prison—the largest and most secure one in the state of Minnesota, built in 1887. It housed criminals between the ages of twenty and thirty.

I was twenty years old. So even if I served a full sentence, I would only be incarcerated there until I reached the age of thirty.

I strutted out of the courtroom to show everyone how tough I was.

9

SURVIVING ST. CLOUD

After two years at the St. Cloud Reformatory, I appeared before the parole board. Most of them were people who knew me from Glen Lake and Red Wing, but one face was different. Les Green, an African American, had been a criminal, straightened out his life, gone to school, earned a degree, and was now the head of the parole board.

I saw hardness in his eyes. I was sure I could beguile the others into reducing my sentence. But I sensed this guy wasn't going to be charmed by me.

After staring at me for several seconds, he said, "You are horribly representing the African American population. Do you know that?"

I lowered my head, ashamed. "Yes, sir."

"It is my duty to see that you are punished for your crime. The others here want to reduce your sentence to two years. Hogwash!"

I nodded slowly.

"You will serve seven years, eight months and eighteen days of your ten-year sentence." He leaned forward, and I felt the anger in his voice. "If you mess up during that time, you will serve the entire ten years."

I had been sure the board would reduce my sentence. I stared back at him and shrugged. I didn't want him to know that I cared.

As soon as I got out of orientation, I headed for the cafeteria. I got in the food line. I didn't know the man serving, and he didn't know me.

The server started to give me a piece of chicken that looked burned.

"I don't want that piece. Give me—"

"You take what I give you. You don't choose."

I let loose with a tirade of swear words and ugly names. The people around me laughed.

"You're an idiot." He stared at me with calmness.

Just then, my friend, Big Howard, tapped me on the shoulder. "Come on, Johnny, let's go."

"No way, man, I'm getting my chicken and he won't—"

"The dude ain't gonna give you no chicken."

"Well, I ain't goin' nowhere until he gives me a piece of good, *unburned* chicken."

The guards started to mingle around and Big Howard pulled me aside. "Be cool, Johnny. I'll get you some chicken, man, just don't say nothin' more."

"No, he ain't gonna punk me."

"That's Sanchez. Johnny, that dude's dangerous."

"I don't care. He's just a Mexican or something so why you afraid of him? There ain't but ten of 'em in the whole penitentiary."

"No, man, there's something special about this dude. He's one of the leaders of the Mexican Mafia, from Los Angeles." From the way Big Howard spoke, I understood that I needed to back down.

"All right." I dropped into a seat. A minute later Big Howard brought me a piece of chicken.

The next day Big Howard came to my cell. "You have to apologize to Sanchez."

"Why?"

"Because if you don't, he'll kill you."

"What do you mean?"

"He's bad, Johnny. Real bad. He's been in three different penitentiaries before this one. Every prison he goes to he kills three or four dudes."

"I'm not afraid of—"

"You should be. You insulted him, and the man ain't said nothin' to you. If you don't apologize you gotta watch that dude every day. And if he gets you, we gotta kill him."

"Okay, man, if it means that much to you."

"It does, and it'll probably save your life." Big Howard was like my big brother, always watching out for me. So I had to listen.

With Big Howard by my side, I went to Sanchez and apologized. "I was having a bad day. I shouldn't done said those things to you. It was just chicken, after all."

"Okay."

"We cool?" Big Howard asked.

"Okay." Sanchez turned and limped away.

But I sensed he wasn't okay.

"What's with the limp?" I asked Big Howard.

He shook his head. "You don't know nothin', Johnny. That dude's been stabbed more than sixty times."

―――

The next day, Big Howard and I were outside in the ball diamond when Sanchez started walking across the field. I nudged Big Howard. When I realized he wasn't coming toward me, I ignored him.

Not more than three minutes later, the prison horn blew. All of the prisoners lay face-down, as we'd been instructed to do whenever we heard the horn.

Armed guards raced toward the ball diamond.

When I looked up, I realized that Sanchez had cut a dude's throat. His butcher knife was a foot away.

The guards grabbed Sanchez and hauled him off. He didn't care. He was never going to get out of prison anyway.

I realized I could have been the one he killed. If I hadn't apologized, I would have been less than four hours away from death, but because I did, he went after somebody else.

―――

While I was incarcerated at St. Cloud I earned as much money as I had on the streets. Because I could think fast and was good with numbers, I became an entrepreneur by loan sharking, drug dealing, or providing anything else the inmates needed. I didn't use drugs in prison, so I stayed alert. I had to be if I wanted to stay alive.

Because I had nothing to spend it on, I saved my money and had ways to send it out for friends to keep for me. They knew I'd give them something for doing me that favor. They also knew I wouldn't let them get away with it if they spent even a dollar of it.

On any given day, I walked around with at least $1,000 in my socks. Whenever people from outside came to visit, the guards searched us. So on the rare occasions I had a visitor, I let one of the boys hold the money for me.

Here's how loan sharking works. I started with $100 and loaned it out for $200. As I kept doing that the money multiplied. The only drawback was in collecting, and most of the time that wasn't a problem.

I kept a list of the release dates of other prisoners, and I was careful not to loan money to anyone just before he got out. I didn't lose much, and the most ever I think was $500.

Occasionally, I lost money when guys got in trouble and were taken into protective custody. During their punishment, they stayed locked up and weren't able to mingle with the prison population. They couldn't even use the phone or have visitors.

But if men didn't pay up, my solution was simple: I had my boys hurt them. On a few occasions, I found out where their families lived and sent someone there to threaten them. It was a dirty business. But they knew what they were getting into.

"You shouldn't have borrowed the money if you couldn't pay it back," I'd say. I didn't show mercy. If I did, the others would see me as weak. And I couldn't let my guard down the whole time I was at St. Cloud.

10

THE BLACK BROTHERHOOD CULTURAL DEVELOPMENT ORGANIZATION

A t St. Cloud, I had no control over my life. Unlike Glen Lake and Red Wing, this was a real prison—and everything was regulated.

After a few weeks, I figured out how to gain some control over my life—and the lives of others.

St. Cloud housed about a thousand men, most of them white. I counted ten Native Americans, five Mexicans, and two Jews. (The Jews were white, of course, but they were labeled as a separate race.) The black inmates received the worst treatment in prison and, despite their grumbling, they took it. I became angry when I witnessed the situation.

"Why don't you do something?" I asked.

"What can we do?"

I heard that more than once. Their defeatist attitude made me realize they wouldn't do anything to change their treatment.

After thinking about it for several days, I told my cell mate, "I'm going to organize them."

Years earlier, someone had tried to set up a prison book club called the Black Brotherhood Cultural Development Organization. BBCDO hadn't worked out, but reactivating a culturally specific program would make the warden look good.

The Black Brotherhood already had written bylaws. But we could ignore those.

I began speaking with other African American inmates, asking them to join me. I asked everyone, all the way from those with the shortest sentence to the ones who received life without parole.

I don't know if anyone could do that today. But back then, only a few inmates were members of gangs, so pulling everyone together was easy, as they already had a natural inclination to be part of a group.

My main job was to convince them that we had a common foe—anyone who wasn't black.

We were a minority, with fewer than a hundred African Americans in a prison population of nine hundred. "If we join into one force and move together, we can be more powerful than the others because they're not organized."

My first obstacle was that the BBCDO already had officers, and they didn't want to give up their authority. Hardly anyone attended their culture-development sessions, so that made it even easier for me. But I had to convince them to turn their organization over to me.

I knew how to do that. Intimidation and threats always worked in prison.

I chose five lieutenants to go with me to the next BBCDO meeting. They were all incarcerated for murder, which meant that they were respected and feared—especially feared. They had nothing to lose because they were serving life sentences without parole.

At that meeting, I announced, "This is a takeover." My five guys stood, yelled, and demanded change. Those who resisted were beaten. I did nothing, except sit and watch it happen. I needed to be seen as the leader of the BBCDO and the one who ordered the attack.

A guard came in, having heard the commotion. The members of the BBCDO stared at him. One of them yelled, "What you gonna do?"

He shrugged and said nothing.

Before that meeting ended, the old leaders "voluntarily" resigned and we had a special election. To no one's surprise, I was nominated as president and no one opposed me. I was in control.

BBCDO was only the beginning. The prison had dozens of groups, mostly small. I went to the Aryan Brotherhood, the bikers, and the major Spanish groups. Standing before them with my five convicted murderers, I said, "If you stay out of our way, we'll let you survive. Otherwise, we'll crush you."

Other than the Aryan Brotherhood, the white prisoners weren't organized because of their differing philosophies and their unwillingness to cooperate with other Caucasians. They were easy to intimidate. To the head of the Aryan Brotherhood I said, "We gonna stick to ourselves and you stick to yourselves."

"Sounds great, man."

"But if you ever have trouble with someone trying to mess with the Aryan Brotherhood, you come to me." I smiled. I didn't need to add, "And we'll take care of him." It was understood.

My plan worked. While I was at St. Cloud, there wasn't a single race riot. That's significant because the prison had been known for having them regularly. Everything went well, I made money, and I was the undisputed power of the cell blocks.

To make the brotherhood more enticing, I promised potential members, "If you join and stay with me, you'll get gifts of sex from women, all the drugs you want, free long-distance calls, and the best jobs in the penitentiary."

Those weren't empty words. I had already figured out all the angles. For example, a prison-recognized nonprofit organization called Women Helping Offenders had been started years earlier to visit and encourage the prisoners. All I had to do, and it was easy to arrange, was get prostitutes to join the organization.

But I built in one control factor. I personally chose the women. That was no problem because I knew most of the African American prostitutes in South Minneapolis, and they didn't mind coming to the prison every month.

I pulled off everything I had promised—drugs, sex, and even had an office where prisoners had access to a free phone with a WATS line.*

I had the connections to get in all the drugs we wanted. My

---

* WATS, Wide Area Telephone Service, begun by the Bell Telephone system in 1961, enabled businesses to obtain a special line with a flat-rate plan. It continued for about twenty years.

lieutenants strong-armed everybody, so my next step was to make sure no one but us sold drugs.

I insisted on having a black guard, and the prison administration agreed. The one assigned to our area we called Yeager, and I knew I could buy his silence. In exchange for his not "seeing" anyone hand us drugs and not looking when inmates went into a little room and had sex with prostitutes, he earned $1,000 a month.

Because volunteers from Women Helping Offenders were never searched, they brought in about 90 percent of our drugs. We had other sources, such as Yeager, who earned more money than his normal salary by bringing in drugs as well.

We had all the drugs and real whiskey we wanted and often held parties in the middle of the night. We set aside one cell block where we could stay up all night with unlocked cells and only one guard watching three hundred inmates.

Once the new BBCDO was established, we functioned well together. I made sure of it. If a serious dispute broke out, we took over the cell block and every black man had to show up. Even if they were going to be released the next day, they had to be there.

———

I also arranged to have two banquets a year. On those occasions, we had a special meal prepared for the Black Brotherhood Cultural Development Organization. The members' girlfriends or wives could come to the prison for the evening. They brought extra food and, of course, drugs, and they were allowed conjugal privileges.

I knew a group of college girls from St. Cloud who were willing to earn a little extra money (and give me a percentage). They would sneak up to one particular window in our cell block, which we had fixed so the entire window came out. The girls bought alcohol for me, which I sold for a good sum because it was better than the hooch the inmates made.

But the good times didn't last.

11

POWER CHALLENGE

After I had been at St. Cloud about a year, and taken control, I was set up to be killed. A guy named Durel, and his hit man, Lewis Burch, believed that if they killed me, they could gain control of the Black Brotherhood Cultural Development Organization.

Durel put out the word that he wanted to buy a large amount of drugs from me and claimed he had received a lot of money from the outside to pay for them. Even though drugs flowed freely, I couldn't make that kind of arrangement around a lot of people. So I agreed to meet him in a school classroom, where there wouldn't be a guard.

Since I'd never had any trouble, I went alone to meet Durel. One of my lieutenants waited outside to warn us if a guard came our way.

I later discovered that the night before, Durel and Lewis bribed a janitor to leave a couple of knives for them somewhere and Lewis had picked them up. They hid them inside their coats. They knew I didn't carry a knife, so I would be defenseless against two of them.

Durel and his hit man came into the classroom. Lewis was the knife man, but wasn't any good at it because he didn't know how to use it properly in order to kill someone.

Durel and I faced each other, and Lewis stood behind me. While we were discussing the terms, I turned around for some reason. Just then, Lewis pulled out a large knife. But he hesitated. I grabbed one of the nearby chairs and threw it at him. It struck Lewis's arm and the knife went flying.

The noise alerted my friend outside the room and he rushed in. Both of us tackled my two assailants.

Durel pulled out a smaller knife. He jabbed and nicked me. That really made me angry and, ignoring his knife, I hit him repeatedly. By the second blow he dropped the knife, trying to deflect my blows. My lieutenant and I hurt those two men so bad they were taken into protective custody. (Of course, they never told the guards who hurt them.)

I couldn't stop thinking about how lucky I was. If I hadn't turned around when I did, I would have been dead.

Less than a month before the next black banquet, Captain Leonard, the head of the prison guards, told me privately that he'd decided the banquets were a security risk, so he was taking that privilege away from all the groups.

He knew the banquet was part of my reward system for members of the Black Brotherhood. Everyone was excited about it, mostly because the men would see their girlfriends. Captain Leonard grinned as if to say, "See? I win."

Although I saw that gesture as a challenge to my authority, I didn't argue with him. He would have liked that. Instead I said, "The men will be disappointed." And I left.

As soon as I returned to the cell block, I called together the members of the BBCDO for an emergency meeting. By then I had devised a plan to defeat Captain Leonard.

When I told the brotherhood about the cancelation of the banquet, they started yelling and cursing. I let them build up anger for a few minutes, then held up my hands for silence. "I know how to stop him."

They listened intently because nothing I promised had ever failed.

"Tomorrow morning when you wake up, do not say *one* word. Not a word! Don't talk on the phone. Don't talk to a supervisor. Don't talk in the food line or while you're eating. Stay completely quiet all day." I paused to let those words sink in.

At first, they weren't sure what to think of my idea. For those who don't understand prison life, black guys are never quiet. We're loud. We talk and joke all day. That's how we do time. A lot of it's bragging and lying. Even while playing cards we're fighting. No one had ever before asked the blacks to remain absolutely silent.

The only time prisoners got quiet was right before a big riot, which built tension among the guards.

"If I'm the only person who speaks, Leonard will certainly want to question me."

They started to understand my plan. And after a few questions, they agreed.

"One more thing, we need to show we're a united front."

We had choices on what to wear—among our prison clothes. So I instructed each man to wear a white T-shirt, blue jeans, brown boots, and a neatly pressed denim jacket. If every black man except me dressed that way, it would be interpreted as a militant gesture, as if they were going to war.

The men did exactly as I asked. The next morning, when other inmates spoke, they didn't answer. At breakfast, everyone noticed the silence. They did their assigned duties with no talking. By the time we went for our noon meal, still not one black person had spoken. Guards whispered to each other and watched more closely.

An hour before our evening meal, Captain Leonard called me into his office. "What is going on? My guards are nervous, the other inmates are nervous, and some of the inmates are afraid to come out of their cells."

"I can't control what's going to happen."

"What do you mean by that?"

"They're angry because you took away our banquet." I stared right at him and refused to flinch.

He nodded, letting me know he understood.

I smiled as if to say, "See? I won."

He yelled at me and made a few threats, but he knew there was nothing he could do to make the men start talking. So he sent me back to my cell. I told the Black Brotherhood we were getting to the administration.

At dinner, the only talking in the room was extremely quiet, mostly whispers. Even the Aryan Brotherhood and the Mexican gangs were subdued.

As I expected, I received a call to go back to the captain's office. I'd hardly walked into the room before he yelled, "If you don't get those guys talking, I'm going to lock you up!"

"If you lock me up," I said quietly, "I can't control what will happen."

He stared at me. The hardness in his eyes said he would like to torture me. I refused to look away. He paced his office, probably trying to gain control of himself. Then he faced me. "What do you want?"

"I want our banquets back."

He was defeated and he knew it. I think he also knew that if he backed down, that would elevate me even more among the inmates. "Okay," he muttered.

I went back and delivered the news that I had gotten the banquets back for everyone.

One man said, "You're like the Messiah. You delivered."

"Thank you, man. You're bad," said one of the Black Brotherhood members (which was a compliment).

"Anything you want," another yelled out. "We'll follow you to the ends of the earth!"

The next day, prison life was back to normal with the flow of drugs, partying, and gambling. Yes, life was better for me on the inside than it had been when I was free.

Like in childhood games, I was the king of the hill. And, without knowing it, I would soon be toppled.

12

FALSELY ACCUSED

One day, as I walked into a cell where I kept my whiskey hidden before I sold it, I found Jawanza (who had once stuffed an old man inside a washing machine) in that cell with an inmate named Dwane. They were raping an albino kid, who looked like the late comedian Jonathan Winters. Apparently the albino had borrowed money that he couldn't repay, so the two men were raping him as his punishment.

"Help me," the kid cried out.

I turned away. I knew that was wrong, but I did nothing. Because Jawanza and Dwane were a couple of my lieutenants, I didn't want to belittle them in front of the kid.

As I left the room, I said over my shoulder, "I want to talk to you guys afterward." They knew I would see that they were punished. Rape happens in prison, but I didn't approve of it.

The rape was so violent, the kid ended up in the hospital and needed thirty stitches. The administration put the entire penitentiary on lockdown, as they did when any violence of that level occurred.

Later that day, twelve guards escorted the two rapists out of the cell block—six guards to a man.

Recognizing the two men as my lieutenants, I said to my cell mate, "I know what that's about."

Within minutes, six more guards came to my cell. "You are under arrest for rape."

I hadn't done anything, so I wasn't worried. By then I had just under five more years to go on my sentence. The most they could do was charge me with being an accessory after the fact. Or so I thought.

They put me in administrative lockup, which is a nice term for solitary confinement. Some inmates did as many as three years. It's the cruelest form of punishment and it causes some inmates to become psychotic.

Prisoners in solitary have only two privileges. They can write one letter a week and use the phone once a week. They kept me in solitary for almost a year. And I didn't get even those privileges.

But I could handle it. Even in solitary, I still had connections to get drugs such as Thorazine—a narcotic for mentally ill patients. Members of the Black Brotherhood snuck me sleeping drugs twice a week, which enabled me to sleep for two or three days at a time.

When I finally faced the charge of rape, the albino kid told the guards exactly what happened. They kept asking, "Are you sure John Turnipseed didn't participate?"

"No, he didn't."

"How do you know? He might have."

The prison guards wanted to get rid of me, so they worked on the poor kid, confused him, and finally convinced him to implicate me.

They said the case would never go to trial if all three of us made a deal.

"I'm not guilty and I won't plead guilty," I insisted.

"If they convict you," a guard said, "you'll probably stay here until you're an old, old man."

"I'm innocent," I said.

The other two guys wouldn't admit I hadn't participated because they didn't want to plead guilty to rape. Jawanza was already serving a twenty-year sentence for murder. Dwane had been convicted of a previous rape, which got him ten years. In the Minnesota justice system, sentences could be stacked on top of each other. If convicted, Jawanza and Dwane would probably have forty years added to their sentences, so they were willing to take me down with them.

The case was scheduled for trial at Stearns County, an all-white county, which at the time was very racist. All three of us black men were charged with raping the albino kid.

The two men wouldn't clear me. I couldn't speak up. If I did, I'd be called a snitch when I went back, and that would erode all my power. So when a black lawyer visited my cell, I thought I was doomed. I was already in jail for aggravated armed robbery, which wasn't an embarrassment, but rape was, especially raping another man. And I didn't want my parents to hear, "Your son's in prison for rape."

I told the lawyer I wasn't guilty and said, "I refuse to plead guilty." I was sure he didn't believe me. Or maybe he didn't care. He certainly didn't inspire any hope.

On the second day of the trial, lawyers questioned the albino. He said he remembered the event clearly. "John Turnipseed didn't have anything to do with the rape."

The guards knew I was innocent, but they were counting on the kid to say what they told him to.

"Are you sure?" the prosecutor asked.

"When the guards questioned me, they kept suggesting that John participated. And I was mad at him for not helping me, so I was willing to lie." He turned and looked at me. "I'm sorry."

The charges against me were dropped. But the jury found the other two guilty, and they received long sentences.

I went back to the prison population. Although I had been out of circulation for a year, I was still in control because I had chosen good enforcers to carry on in my absence.

But the administration had made changes. Members of Women Helping Offenders were no longer allowed to come to the prison. Stan Hill, whom I hadn't known, had taken over as the president of BBCDO.*

Wanting to get rid of me, the prison authorities sent me to minimum security, even though I didn't fit the guidelines. It was a coed prison, and I could mingle with the women. Life there was easy and soft.

After I had been in minimum security for forty-five days, Les Green, the head of the parole board who didn't like me, visited me. "I could have you home in half an hour."

"What are you talking about?" I asked.

---

* Years later, Stan started to work for me as manager of on-the-job training at the Center for Fathering. He is still there.

"You can be released."

"I still have four years left."

"You have three and a half years. And if you can forget about what happened with the false charges, you'll get out on parole now."

I stared at him, not believing what I had just heard.

He explained that because the guards had forced the albino to lie about me, the parole board was willing to release me.

"Deal!"

Just like that. I was a free man. Instead of doing seven years for a ten-year conviction, I was out in less than four.

———

While I was still in prison, I met Madupie Edwards, one of the older women with Women Helping Offenders. She became one of the leaders that brought in prostitutes. She liked me and did a number of nice things for me.

Even though I was in maximum security at the time, she pulled off one special deal. She arranged with Captain Leonard for me to leave the prison under escort for a modeling assignment in Minneapolis. And they brought me back that same evening.

The modeling event, held at Dayton's Department Store (at that time the largest store of its kind in Minneapolis) hosted the event to raise money for Women Helping Offenders.

Madupie dressed me in a red suit with a red polka-dotted tie. I walked down the runway with an attractive woman from the prison who wore an expensive gown. The event provided a nice break from prison life.

Madupie Edwards liked me. She was too old for me, but she was gorgeous and I liked her. She had shot and killed her husband, a well-known musician named Frank Lyle, who used to beat her. She never had to serve time.

"I want you to be with my daughter, Kay," Madupie told me that day in Dayton's. "She's a prostitute and she'll work for you when you get out."

Kay had been forced into prostitution by her boyfriend, whom

Madupie hated. "He beats her. But if she goes with you, I know you won't beat her."

"Okay," I said, and agreed to meet Kay after I was released.

Handing over a daughter for a man to pimp sounds horrible to most people—and it is—but in the culture Madupie and I came from, it happened all the time.

After my release, Madupie introduced me to her daughter. The boyfriend-pimp was there, but he left. I think he was afraid of me.

Kay was even prettier than her mother, and she was glad to go with me. She introduced me to her friends, and they also wanted to work for me. So just that easy, I became a full-fledged pimp with five girls.

Then the unexpected happened. I fell in love with Kay.

13

FALLING IN LOVE

Not only did I fall in love with Kay, I also married her in 1979. She continued in prostitution. Soon after our wedding, Kay told me she was pregnant. Since I was the only man who had unprotected sex with her, I knew I was the father.

I had to accept that responsibility. However, being a career criminal, I didn't sign the birth certificate because I didn't want to pay child support.

Kay continued as a prostitute, our son became a welfare kid, and I remained a thief and a gambler—a thug. Everybody was all right with the arrangement. It seemed normal.

About the time I became a pimp, I saw a well-known pimp named Little Richard who said, "Turnipseed, if you're going to stay in this business, you've got to think, 'Kill the baby and sell the blood,' because a pimp's gotta live."

Sell the blood meant we had to be so ruthless that we didn't care about anything. We could even drain blood from the dead and sell it.

"Don't allow your girls to get pregnant," he said. "But if they do, make sure they have an abortion the next day." He wasn't referring to a legal procedure in a sterile hospital, but a cheap abortion in some back room.

"Make sure your women work seven days a week. Don't give them a break. If you're not willing to do that, you're not going to make a good pimp."

I believed him. And that meant I had to learn to become cruel and unfeeling. To be a successful pimp I had to send somebody's daughter out on the street twenty times a day.

So I did it. For a while.

Sometimes I'd meet a runaway, be kind to her, and then set her up with drugs. I'd go out and tell men, "For ten dollars apiece, you can come inside for five minutes." The girl would be so drugged she wouldn't know what was happening. And that broke her into the business. Even if she ran away the next day, I'd have earned $2,000.

Those of us who were lucky picked up two or three runaways in one night, and there were always plenty of men who would pay. Some of the perverts would even buy a girl for the whole night. All I had to do was supply them with a girl and a room.

One important thing I learned: A man can't be a pimp and have a conscience. I had to rip it out and throw it away. Otherwise, my actions would have been too painful. At times, guilt and remorse came back, but having more dope helped me to kill those emotions again. And I had plenty of people around to keep me focused.

Most of the guys I hung around and idolized were pimps—the scum of the earth. Contrary to the way the movies usually portray them, pimps are violent. I always had to remind myself that they have to be, and always be ready to fight. And to my shame, I admired that toughness and their dominance over people. They viewed women as female dogs. I had to take on that attitude myself. To think any different would make me weak.

It wasn't unusual for us pimps to steal each other's women. We'd slip a drug into their drinks and they'd wake up in another state. They were already prostitutes, and to our hardened ways, it didn't seem to make any difference who pimped them.

Once in a while, one of my girls would get violently assaulted sexually.

One night, two men tried to kidnap my first wife, Kay, who was still a prostitute. She was working the bar and two black guys kept on wanting to buy her drinks. I didn't mind. I sat at a table far enough away that I wasn't noticed, but close enough so I could watch them.

When Kay almost passed out, the two men started to escort her outside. I knew what they doing—it was the same thing I had done to other prostitutes.

But I yelled, "Hey! What are you doing?"

They ran out of the bar.

I took Kay home. The thought of what she could have gone through that night was too much for me to bear. Yes, it's strange because when I was pimping my wife, I didn't think about it. But having two other pimps try to steal her made me realize what a cruel, heartless thing I was doing.

———

Kay and I had a son, whom we named Shaun Ramone Eason. After Kay recovered from childbirth, she went back to prostitution.

Most of her dates came to our house. If I was home during those times, I'd go into the other bedroom while they had sex. She'd finish, take a shower, and it would be over. If I had to be away from home, we hired a babysitter.

She had a standing date with a middle-aged man. About six months after Shaun's birth, Kay paged me—this was in the day before cell phones. When I called her, she said, "The babysitter didn't show up. You have to watch Shaun while I turn this date."

"Okay," I said reluctantly. Babysitting wasn't a man's job, but I didn't know what else to do.

By the time her date arrived, I was already in the other room with Shaun. The noises didn't bother me, but whenever Kay made a sound, Shaun would turn his head.

About the fifth time it happened, I became so upset I walked out, slammed the door, and barged into our bedroom. "Get out of my house!" I yelled at the man. "And don't come back!"

He was too frightened to argue. He hurriedly got dressed and ran out of the house.

As soon as he was gone, I said to Kay, "I don't want you in that lifestyle anymore. You're going to school."

"How are we going to pay the bills?"

"I'll take care of us." I was in love with her, and I didn't want her to be a prostitute anymore.

My conscience came alive and I couldn't shut it up. The next day, I went to each of my girls and set them free. Most of them went with other pimps, but at least I didn't have to dominate them. I couldn't stand treating women that way any longer.

One of the prostitutes was living with us. When she came back to the house that night, I kicked her out.

"What did I do?"

"Nothing. Just go. Find another pimp. I don't care. I don't want any more prostitutes."

After she left, I held my son and gazed at the woman I loved. The only way I could think of to take care of my responsibility was to increase the number of my robberies. Because I was now over eighteen, if I were caught using a gun I would be tried as an adult with a stiffer sentence. I wasn't ready to leave a life of crime, but I had to change my method.

"I'm going to focus on business burglaries," I told Kay. "That will take care of us." That style of crime appealed to me because I liked wearing suits and could talk my way past security guards. More important, there was a lot of money in targeting businesses—much more than household robberies.

In my new life of crime, I broke into drug stores for the drugs and jewelry stores for goods that were easy to fence. Not only was I back into crime, but I was even more into drugs. As my habit increased, I needed even more income.

After about a year of snorting more and more cocaine, someone introduced me to mainlining—shooting it into my arms or other body parts. The sensation was euphoric. It was the most exciting and the most devastating thing that had ever happened to me. As far as drugs are concerned, none can compare to mainlining.

During the first weeks of mainlining, I injected myself about ten times a day. I knew people who said they'd done it fifty times in a day.

Each time I stuck the needle in a different place on my body so no one would notice track marks on my arms, like you saw on a lot of addicts.

When I came down from mainlining, all I wanted to do was sleep—but it also brought on deep depression, worse than anything I'd ever known. Yet I kept going back to feel that tremendous high. When I crashed, as always happened, I'd say, "I don't want to feel like this." I was so miserable, I wondered why I shouldn't just kill myself. Then I'd say, "The only way I can fix this is to get high again." That was the pattern of my daily life.

Drugs weren't new to me, but, like many other criminals, I had moved on to bigger, more powerful drugs. All forms of cocaine effectively made me euphoric.

Snorting cocaine, which is where I started, is the weakest form of the drug. When I snorted, I spent about $100 a day. The next step is smoking crack (made by treating the hydrochloride of cocaine with sodium bicarbonate to create small chips used for smoking) which I, and probably a lot of others, did instead of snorting. Crack costs more than snorting. And mainlining is the most expensive, but nothing compared with the ultimate ecstasy I experienced. But after the bigger high came agitation, depression, and paranoia.

In those days, mainlining cost me twenty-five dollars an injection. And I shot up a minimum of eight times a day, sometimes as many as fifteen. *Every day.*

Despite the extra thrill from mainlining, I got tired of needles. Dull ones hurt. I had to keep going to the drugstore and getting new ones. Unlike others, I had gone from snorting straight to mainlining. But after about two years of shooting up, a woman turned me on to crack. Crack was less expensive than mainlining cocaine, but I could stay high for several days. It also got me out of using needles.

I did an amazing number of petty crimes to support myself, my wife, my son, and my drug habit. One big moneymaker was to run after-hour parties once the bars closed. At the parties, people bought sex, alcohol, and drugs. They'd also gamble. In those days, the police never came into our area. And I made money—a lot.

I could buy a bottle of cheap whiskey for five dollars and sell it for two or three dollars a drink. After three drinks I had earned back my investment.

People who drink also want food. So I'd buy a hundred chicken dinners and sell them for more than double what I'd paid for them.

If the partygoers wanted girls, I rented them a room for $200.

Dice games also paid off. Each bet cost twenty-five cents. Every time a point was thrown, I took a portion of the money—one or two dollars. It added up. I made up to $4,000 off of one dice game.

———

Occasionally we had problems. In one house, a man came in with $6,000. A friend and I tricked him with funny (loaded) dice so there was no way he could win. After we had taken almost all his money, he threw the dice again. One die looked like it was going to turn over, then it moved in slow motion before flipping back over.

"Hey, what's this?" He picked up the die, examined it, and threw it repeatedly. Each time the same number came up.

We intended to use the trick dice for only two rolls, then go back to regular dice. But in our excitement, we forgot to make the switch.

The stranger started yelling and making wild threats. My friend grabbed him, beat him real bad, and threw him outside on the sidewalk.

That was our second mistake.

Less than twenty minutes after we tossed the guy out, a gang of at least thirty men surrounded the house. (Apparently, down the street a crowd had been having a birthday party, and the cheated man had left them to gamble with us.) Some went to the front door and kicked it. One person shot the door. My friend and I had guns, but two people weren't enough against so many, so we called the police.

As more people gathered, my partner in crime screamed, "I didn't do anything. It was Johnny Turnipseed!"

When they heard the police sirens, several in the group shot through the window a few times and then hurried away. If they had gotten inside, they would certainly have killed us.

So that was another time that I should have died.

14

STUPID MISTAKES

In those days, a lot of money came in, but I spent even more. I splurged on cars, clothes, anything I wanted. No matter how carelessly I handled money, I was careful about three things: paying my friends, taking care of my son and my brothers, and giving Mom money for Lisa.

Kay worked as a grocery store clerk while she struggled through school. She earned her GED and went on to Minneapolis Business College. Still working the system, she received loans and scholarships and we spent the money on other things.

One day, an attractive woman lured me over to St. Paul. Although Minneapolis and St. Paul are called the Twin Cities, a bridge over the Mississippi River separates them. Previously, I had beaten up some guys who had friends in the mob in St. Paul, so it was stupid and dangerous for me to go over there.

The lady and I went to a place where we gambled, and I did reasonably well. After a couple of hours, I stepped outside. Just then, someone shoved a gun in my face."

"What's going on?" I asked.

The man, whose face I couldn't see in the dark, didn't answer. He and two others guys hit me quite a few times—heavy hits.

"What do you want?"

They didn't answer, but they searched me and took every cent I had, including the $1,000 I kept in my socks, which gave them a total of about $4,000.

Finally, they stopped beating me. One of them came up close so I could see his face. "Remember me?"

"Yeah, I do."

"Now it's my turn. And we're going to kill you."

"Hey, come on, we can settle this—"

"Shut up!" He slugged me and yelled, "Get in the trunk!"

A car pulled up right next to us. The driver was the woman who'd brought me there.

It suddenly dawned on me that she must be working for these guys. She'd notified them I was at the gambling house, and they had been waiting for me to come out.

"I said, get in!"

"Okay, okay." I crawled into the trunk. To my surprise, no one tied me up. If the roles had been reversed, that's what I would have done to him.

While inside the trunk, I made no noise. It wouldn't have done any good. I lay there quietly, trying to figure out how to survive. My instincts said, When the trunk opens, jump out screaming.

I twisted my body around so I would be ready to leap out feet first. After what seemed like half an hour, the car stopped and the doors slammed. Someone opened the trunk. I kicked him aside as I jumped out, and ran as fast as I could. My bold action took them by surprise. One of them shot at me, but he missed me in the dark.

About a block away I flagged down a car. "Help me! Some bad guys are shooting at me."

"Hop in," the driver said, and away we went. Again, wearing a suit paid off.

As we drove, I thought about the man who had threatened me. I didn't recall his name, but I remembered what happened. He had come to one of my craps houses, and within minutes he showed a bad attitude. Every time he lost, he grumbled and made a lot of noise. After a while, I got tired of his complaints.

"That's enough," I said, and slugged him.

One of my friends joined me and we beat him pretty bad. We half-carried him to his car and put him inside.

"Don't come back." I leaned down close to his face. "Next time it will be worse."

As I thought about that incident, I realized how lucky I was to be alive. It never occurred to me that God might have had something to do with my escape.

———

Everything was going well for me, and I was living the high life. I had all the money and drugs I wanted. Even though I was married to Kay and loved her, I still had three or four girlfriends. They regularly gave me money, which was part of our culture. Girlfriends often supported the men in their lives. Some of my girls were prostitutes, but most were women with jobs. And each one said I was *her man.*

I was an attractive man who looked clean and dressed well. I'd learned early on that if I made a woman feel like she was the equivalent of a female dog I could get anything I wanted from her. Each of those women was somebody's daughter, and I didn't want my daughter treated that way. But I didn't let my mind dwell on those thoughts.

One girlfriend, Tangie, worked two jobs. She gave me all the money from one job and she kept what she made on the other one. She liked me a lot. I saw her once a week—on payday, of course.

Despite my criminal history, and regularly being on probation or parole, I tried to work legal jobs. I really did, but the money was too little to fit my lifestyle. For a month or so, I cleaned machines at the Munsingerwear factory. But it was manual labor. And I wasn't a manual labor type. Each day I went to work, I hated the job more. But what other kind of job was there for an uneducated man like me?

When I broke my hand on one of the machines at Munsingerwear, I said, "That's it. I quit."

I'd tried to go straight. But even when I had a real job, I still stole, and not just because I needed the money. What thrill was there in sweeping floors or polishing machines? I missed the danger and adrenaline flow.

My crimes increased, but I stayed away from banks and credit cards because they were too dangerous and created too many problems.

Stealing from businesses was much easier. I went to work after they closed.

Here's an example of the new way I worked. First, I'd steal a couple of shirts with the word *Janitor* written above the front pocket. Then I decided which office I wanted to rob. Sometime during the day, while dressed like a janitor, I walked into the building. Guards glanced at me, but because I looked and acted the part, they nodded for me to go forward.

I strolled through the building and located the offices I wanted to hit. Sometimes I emptied wastebaskets, all the while observing and listening. Since no one paid any attention to me, it was easy to find out what I needed to know.

That evening, I'd come back wearing a suit, a white dress shirt, and an expensive tie. Since I looked like I worked there, no guards ever stopped me.

I was good at this. But I almost got caught twice. Police officers would arrest me just on suspicion. Even though they questioned me, and were sure I was guilty, they never had enough evidence to charge me.

"I'm too smooth for them," I boasted to myself.

I started targeting businesses that had equipment I could sell or ones that kept a lot of cash in the office. In the early days of computers, hard drives were expensive. I found a man who would buy them from me for $100. For a couple of years, that became my specialty. I could open a computer and steal the hard drive in less than two minutes. Then I'd close it back up so no one would know until they tried to use the computer. Most people didn't have a clue as to why the computer wasn't working. It never occurred to them that they had no hard drive.

One time I went to an office early in the morning, wearing a nice suit. I bent over and began dismantling a computer.

A woman walked in. "What are you doing?"

"Your computer has a virus. All the computers here do. I'm fixing them."

"Who do you work for?"

"IBM."

"Oh. Well, thank you."

"It's going to take me a while, so you might as well go home. The computers won't be up anytime this morning."

"I didn't get a message about that."

I lowered my voice and said confidentially, "We think the virus was planted by one of the workers here. That's why I'm here so early." I smiled before I said, "There was no reason to alarm you. But we're taking precautions." I stood up so she could look me over.

She smiled at me. "Thank you for being so discreet."

I was interrupted no more than ten times. But once during my business burglary career, a technician caught me and asked, "Who are you?"

I gave him my quick spiel and added, "The authorization to do this came from higher up. I'm not at liberty to say who. You need to talk to your boss. He may be allowed to tell you."

He stared at me. For a second, I thought he was going to call my bluff.

"Look, we think some bad things are going on. So we're putting in some security measures to stop them."

The expression on his face changed. I could tell he believed me.

I inched a little closer. "I probably shouldn't have told you that much. Please . . . don't get me in any trouble."

"I won't. I promise." And he left the office.

Another time, I stole twenty new laptops. The security guard saw me in my suit, pushing a cart I had also taken from the office. "Need any help?" he asked.

"That's nice of you."

While he unknowingly assisted me with the robbery, I acted confidently, and friendly. I even talked with him about sports. He didn't write down my license or ask any questions.

Once in a while I'd try to do a job while I was high. The drugs made me feel invulnerable, so I often ended up doing something dumb, like forgetting to put on a suit. When someone encountered me, the cocaine had me so frazzled I took off running.

It was stupid. But when I was high on drugs, stupid was normal.

15

BIG FRANK

One of my favorite areas for burglary was nursing homes. Because I had no conscience, I'd steal heirlooms, wedding rings, diamonds, broaches—anything that looked expensive. I hit nursing homes in affluent areas where no one expected to be robbed. After all, they had safes and people on duty at the entrance. As if that was enough security to keep me out.

By wearing a suit, I could go in and do whatever I wanted. When people on duty saw a confident, clean-shaven male dressed in an expensive suit, they didn't question him. I ignored the person at the desk, went directly into an office, and closed the door. It took me only seconds to get into the safe.

Back then, doors were flimsy and safes were cheap.

———

The police would charge you with burglary if you were caught wearing gloves, so I never wore them. Instead, I learned to touch things in a way that left no fingerprints, like wrapping a napkin around my hand. I didn't carry a toolbox or anything else. But I kept a screwdriver in my sleeve. I put the stolen goods in my coat pockets and calmly walked out.

On the few times when the police caught and searched me, not once did they pat down my sleeves and discover my screwdriver.

In 1980, when robbing a business office, I used a screwdriver to trip the lock, but when I slid a window open, I inadvertently left a thumbprint. But I wasn't too worried. The police had about a million fingerprints on file, and they had to manually compare each one. They'd probably give up long before they found a match for mine.

What I didn't know was that the police department had recently installed a new computer. By running my thumbprint through their database, they identified me quickly.

A detective called me in, and because I was on parole, I had to talk to him. I walked into the station feeling carefree, certain I'd be out within minutes. He showed me a picture of the business I had burglarized less than a week earlier. "You ever been here?"

"I have never been in that place in my life."

He held up a document. "Well, John, this is the thumbprint the burglar left in that office." He held up a second sheet. "And here's your print." He smiled. "But if you've never been there then that must not be yours."

"I'm through talking." I had already said too much by denying I had been there. That proved that I was a liar.

"Congratulations, John. You're the first person we've caught by computerized fingerprints in the State of Minnesota." I didn't know if that was true, but it didn't matter. He added, "And we plan to use that evidence at your trial."

They charged me with two burglaries. Apparently, on the same night I committed my crime, somebody else went into an office a couple of floors above and stole $8,000.

"I did not commit two burglaries," I insisted. "If you take one of them away, I'll confess to the other."

"We're not taking one away."

"Then I'm not pleading guilty." That must sound like a strange kind of ethics, but I couldn't bring myself to confess to a crime I hadn't done.

At the trial, the judge read the charges, laid them aside, and stared at me. "Mr. Turnipseed, do you seriously want to walk away from two years and get five?"

"I didn't do that second robbery, and I don't want it on my record." That was a big mistake, but my ego was too involved.

The case went to jury trial, and they didn't believe me. Because I had a prior conviction for home invasion, that made me a felon.

The judge gave me a five-year sentence in the Minnesota Correction

Facility at Stillwater in Bayport, Washington County. It was my second time in prison.

"Your life is in danger, Turnipseed," the warden said. "If you want, I can put you in protective custody."

"What kind of danger am I in?"

"The rumor is that you were a snitch. The prisoners blame you for Big Frank being in here."

I remembered Big Frank. I'd met him when I was running a craps game in a small room with only one door. The window was padlocked so no one could sneak in or out.

Big Frank was a frequent player and often won some money. But one night, he lost every time he threw the dice. The more he lost, the angrier he became. He was swearing and yelling so much, I should have realized he was ready to explode.

Finally, Big Frank pulled out a pistol—a big one. "I want my money back."

"I ain't givin' you nothin'," I said, even though I knew he'd already killed three or four people.

The others in the room, aware that something was going to happen, snuck out. I was sitting at one end of a big table. Big Frank couldn't see my hands . . . or those of my cousin Debarr, who was sitting on the opposite end.

Big Frank kept yelling at me, but I stayed calm. "You lost, Big Frank. That's how craps works, and why it's called gambling."

"I'm gonna kill you." The hardness of his face left no doubt that he wasn't making an idle threat.

"Wait a minute," I said, trying to keep my voice calmer than I felt. "Let's talk about this."

Debarr, from his side of the table, was swearing and yelling.

Instead of calming down, Big Frank became even more irritable. He kept turning his head so he could keep an eye on both me and Debarr. I couldn't move—I couldn't even duck. And I didn't think I could effectively shoot through the heavy table.

Suddenly Big Frank turned to my cousin and shot him in the face. Debarr fell to the floor, his head covered with blood. As he fell, he knocked over the bucket of money. It spilled, and a lot of the dollar bills fell into the pool of his blood.

I figured I was going to die, so I raised my gun to shoot Big Frank. Before I could pull the trigger, he turned and ran from the room.

Debarr was dead and Big Frank was gone, so I bent down to scoop up the money.

"Johnny . . . help me," Debarr choked out in a weak voice.

I needed to rush him to the hospital, but I wasn't going to leave all that money. If I did, someone would grab it before I got back. Hurriedly, I stuffed blood-soaked bills into my pockets. Then I grabbed Debar, and carried him to my car. Ignoring all speed limits I rushed him to the hospital's emergency entrance. I told the receptionist that I had a man who'd been shot in the face and he was bleeding real bad.

Two men wheeled out a gurney and brought Debarr inside. I tried to leave, but the guard on duty stopped me. Just then, my cousin told the guard, "Big Frank shot me, and Johnny knows his real name."

Which I did. But I wouldn't tell no matter how many times they asked.

Within hours, the police had identified Big Frank.

Big Frank believed I was willing to testify against him, and knew he'd get a lesser sentence if he pleaded guilty. So he confessed. When he went to prison, he spread the word among his friends that I was a snitch. Because of that, some inmates believed I had been sent to prison to be a snitch there.

When Big Frank heard I had been sentenced to Stillwater, he told the other inmates, "Just wait until Johnny gets here. I'll take care of him."

When I arrived, the other prisoners were waiting to see what would happen. They were expecting something like a shootout at the O.K. Corral.

"I don't want protective custody," I told the warden.

"Your choice," he said, but I could tell from his voice he believed I was making a big mistake.

In the black culture, if they call a man Big Frank, he's a big guy. If we call someone Tiny, it's because he's small. The same with monikers like Killer or Long Mouth.

On my first day, an older prisoner brushed by me and said, "Don't try nothin' in here or we'll kill you."

No one had ever talked to me like that, and I wondered what he meant. Just then, Big Frank came toward me. I smiled and held out my hand.

Instead of shaking it, he glared at me. A friend, who was as large as Big Frank, was with me or I might have been attacked right then.

"Wait until your friend's not around," Big Frank muttered.

My friend took a step toward Big Frank, but I stopped him. "Don't. Just chill." I turned to Big Frank. "Why are you mad at me?"

"You told on me. You're a snitch!"

"I didn't tell anyone on you!"

"Yes, you did! That's why I confessed."

Trying to sound calm, I said, "Do you have a statement?"

"Yeah."

"Then go back and read it before you accuse me."

Big Frank left, still furious. Within minutes he was back, holding up a paper. "I got it! Right here it says that John Turnipseed said—"

"No, not that. If I had snitched," I said, "I would have had to *sign* a statement. You won't find one with my signature on it because I didn't speak up against you."

He turned away in anger and yelled over his shoulder, "I'll find out. I'm gonna call my attorney." Big Frank was a man with a lot of money and he had hired his own lawyer. He called the man who then contacted the police.

"Okay, you didn't do it," Big Frank said afterward, and cussed out the detective who had lied to him. "My lawyer said there was no such statement from you and the detective admitted that he lied to get me to confess."

That story has a happy ending for Big Frank. Because the detective lied, Big Frank received a new trial and his sentence was overturned.

I escaped death once again, with my reputation intact.

That night, I didn't sleep well, knowing that Big Frank could have taken my life without talking to me. I kept thinking about what a mess my life had become. I knew I needed to straighten out, but I also realized I didn't have the strength of character to do that. *Maybe it would have been better if he had. I hate my life and I hate myself.*

As I lay there, I distinctly remember thinking, I could have gone straight to hell on a freeway pass. And I don't care.

16

ALMOST KILLED

While I was incarcerated, Art Erickson, whom I'd ignored and walked away from many times, proved the kind of man he was. With the help of members of the Park Avenue Methodist Church, he saw that my family had food. That would have amazed me, except that I knew Art was that kind of man. And later, I would realize it even more.

I have to tell another story that happened the year I went to Stillwater.

Before my conviction, Jeffrey Steigel, the head of a gang of killers, came to one of my gambling houses to shoot craps. The more he lost, the angrier he became. He was carrying a lot of money that day, and within an hour, had lost everything.

"I'll be back." He left, and within an hour, Jeffrey was back with a big wad of bills. His return reminded me of the days when I'd go out and do a fast robbery for more gambling money.

I pointed to some of the bills, which had blood on them. "Man, did you stick somebody up?"

"What's it to you?" Jeffrey started cussing me out.

"I don't know what you're on, but chill out," I said. I could see trouble coming, so I laid my pistol on my lap, under the table.

"I ain't gonna chill out," Jeffrey said. "Who you think you is?"

My cousin, seated at the far end of the table said, "That's Johnny Turnipseed, man. We all good. We all in the same thing."

"Oh, yeah? Well, I'm into stick-ups." He showed me his big gun and I showed him mine. And we became friends—as much as we could, being criminals.

Shortly after that, Jeffrey and his friend Johnny Gaskin came to my house. Johnny had previously been dating Debbie, a woman in the neighborhood. Since he'd just gotten out of prison, he came looking for her.

"Where's my woman?" Johnny demanded.

"Who's your woman?"

"Debbie."

"Debbie's not my woman," I said.

"Where is she? I want her."

I'd had a casual affair with Debbie and knew where she lived. "I'll take you to her."

Johnny and I got into my car and I drove him to Debbie's house. Just as Johnny walked up to the front door, Debbie's dad, a big man, rushed out, and stabbed Johnny Gaskin in the throat with a pair of scissors.

I raced up the porch steps. The scissors were still in Johnny's neck, and Debbie's dad was wiggling them around to kill him. I pulled out my pistol and pushed it against the father's head. "Stop!"

He let go, shrugged, and walked back inside the house.

I grabbed Johnny, glad to realize he was still alive, carried him to my car, and raced him to the hospital. On the way, he handed me a big wad of money tied with four or five rubber bands. "If I live, I want my money back. If I die, bury me and keep the rest."

"Cool. I'll take care of it."

At the time I had plenty of money. So after I left the hospital, I put Johnny's money inside a bag and tossed it into my trunk.

About a week later, Johnny was out of the hospital, but his neck was taped and he looked terrible. He knocked on my door.

I opened it, and before I had a chance to say anything, Johnny asked, "You got my money?"

"I got it." We walked out to my car, I popped the trunk, opened the bag, and pulled out his wad of money. I handed it to him.

"We're friends, man." He shook my hand and left.

Months later, we were both at a gambling house (not one of ours), and Johnny got mad at everybody, probably because he was losing big time. He yelled to me, "Leave!"

"What? Why?"

"Just leave."

I did.

I stood outside, trying to figure out what was going on in there.

A few minutes later, Johnny casually walked outside. We got into his car. Looking back at the house, I saw flames devouring the building. Everyone from inside raced out. They were all naked, and some were burned bad.

"Let's go," he said, and drove off.

That's when I realized how ruthless Johnny Gaskin was.

———

Johnny Gaskin and Jeffrey, with their gang from Gary, Indiana, joined up with me and we did a few robberies together. But I wasn't comfortable working with Johnny because of his quick temper and his brutal behavior. I'd heard a rumor that while robbing the Jolly Troll Smorgasbord, he killed someone just because the guy protested over getting robbed. I don't know any details, but somehow Johnny beat the rap.

A couple of men from the FBI came to see me one day, saying Johnny and Jeffrey had murdered somebody during a robbery. I wasn't with them when it happened. But since they knew I ran with them, they questioned me about it.

"I don't know anything about that," I said.

Ordinarily, I would have told Jeffrey or Johnny about the incident, but for some reason, I didn't.

The FBI agents knew Johnny Gaskin had been dating Debbie, and they called on her as well. One of them said, "Johnny told me to tell you it's okay to tell us about the murder."

"What? Johnny wouldn't do that—"

"Well, this time he did. He said to tell us everything you know."

"Which Johnny said that?"

Since they wouldn't tell her whether it was Johnny Gaskin or me, she refused to tell them anything.

Not long afterward, both Johnny and Jeffrey were caught for another crime and sentenced to Stillwater prison. During one of her visits to Johnny, Debbie told him about the FBI's visit.

In 1980, I also was sentenced to Stillwater.

My first morning there, when the cell doors opened to let us out for breakfast, Johnny Gaskin and Jeffrey rushed into my cell—so quickly it was blur. A third man came in right behind them. They grabbed my bed sheets, and wrapped them around me, forming a type of straitjacket.

I couldn't move. But I didn't cry out because it wouldn't have done any good.

Jeffrey pulled out a big knife and pushed it against my throat.

"Did the FBI come to see you?" Johnny asked.

"Sure, but I didn't tell them anything."

Gaskin stepped so close, I felt his breath on my face. "You saved my life once. Right now I'm saving yours. We're even."

I nodded.

"If the FBI or police ever come talk to you," he said, stepping closer, "and you don't tell me, I'm gonna kill you."

Jeffrey grinned, and I could see he wanted Johnny to kill me. "You did a good deed, and now he's doing you one. It's a good exchange." He put the knife away. "But watch your back."

I'd been shot, stabbed, and thrown into a trunk, but I had never experienced that type of rage. And I had never been so scared.

17

STILLWATER AND DAN TAYLOR

Before Stillwater, my brothers, little cousins, and I had been tagged the "crash crew" because we bullied people all over South Minneapolis. Now that I was off the scene, other gangs started doing things they would have been afraid to try if I were around.

One violent pimp ran off with my wife, Kay, and our son, Shaun. Even though I was in prison, he knew it wasn't safe for him to stay in Minneapolis because the Bloods would kill him. So he left the state.

As I later found out, a second pimp stole Kay and my son from him and took them to Oklahoma, where he put Kay to work for him.

That wasn't unusual. Pimps stole women from other pimps all the time. I had done it several times myself during that phase of my criminal career. But it didn't stop there.

That pimp was what I call vicious and hardcore. He didn't like sitting with my son while Kay was out on the streets. He wasn't a patient man, and he regularly beat Shaun.

In 1981, the pimp hit Shaun in the head so violently, the boy's brain swelled and he died. He beat Kay that night as well.

When I heard the news, it broke my heart. Again, I thought of the way my own father had treated my mother and the violence I witnessed. Dad didn't beat me, but if he had, I wondered if, like Shaun, I would have died.

Later, I learned that the doctor had told the police, "Dying was probably the best thing for him because that man systematically beat the baby day after day."*

Because I was Shaun's father (even though the records didn't show it), prison officials from Oklahoma called me for permission to "take him off" (to bury him.) I hadn't seen Kay in a year and they didn't give me any details except to say Shaun was dead. I insisted on seeing him.

"That's not going to happen, Mr. Turnipseed."

But four days later, they brought Shaun's body back to South Minneapolis for his funeral. To my surprise, a guard called me out of my cell. He took me to the funeral, still in chains. I don't know how the preacher pulled it off, but he received permission for me to attend.

When I trudged into the funeral home, my shackles clanged with every step. When I saw my mother and grandmother, I hung my head in shame. My godly grandmother had predicted I would be a preacher, and instead, I was in chains. I couldn't look her in the face.

Shamed and grieving, I couldn't hold back the tears.

Although the shackles prevented me from lifting my hands, I walked up to my father to hug him. I leaned toward him.

Dad pulled away and pushed me toward Mom.

He had never hugged me before, and never shown me any love. Why did I think he would be different now? I didn't reason it out, but he was the wrong person to turn to. My crying increased and I couldn't even wipe away my own tears.

My mother hugged me, and then she wiped my face with a tissue. Grandmother hugged me too. I kept mumbling, "I'm sorry, so sorry." I didn't know if she understood what I meant.

I went to the casket to see the body of my dead son. Someone had put a skull cap on Shaun because his head was so messed up. They couldn't make it look normal.

For a minute or two, the tears flowed freely and I didn't care. Shaun was my son and I had failed him in every way. I had deserted him, just like my father had deserted me.

As I left the casket, I stopped crying. Then I became mad at

---

* He received a sentence of eighty years in an Oklahoma prison. After seven years he hung himself.

myself, thinking how stupid I had been. Had I not been so broken up, I wouldn't have tried to embrace him. Dad had never hugged me before, so why would he start now?

It was a dark time in my life, but it would get darker before I saw the light.

———

At first, I blamed God for Shaun's death because that was easy. But as time wore on, I realized that God had nothing to do with the terrible events of my life. The Lord wasn't going to smile at me just because I created Shaun Turnipseed.

I hurt inside—the kind of pain I couldn't explain to anyone.

And it didn't stop, even after I was back at Stillwater. I became suicidal. But I couldn't take my life because in our culture, suicide is considered cowardly, and destroys any legacy or reputation a person might have built. So I turned to the only painkiller I knew: heavy dosages of drugs.

Twice I overdosed enough to kill myself. But I didn't die.

Finally I made a decision: When I get out of Stillwater I'm going straight. Many convicts say that while they're incarcerated, but I truly meant it.

Then.

———

Prison was lonely, even though I had people around me all the time. But I needed something more—someone to really care about me, although I wouldn't have admitted it.

In desperation to talk to someone from the outside, I signed up with a Minnesota non-profit organization called Amicus (Latin for *friend*), which attempts to build relationships between offenders, volunteers, and the community. A Caucasian named Dan Taylor volunteered to meet me. A highly educated man, Dan was a college professor and a Christian. He looked like the actor who portrayed Grizzly Adams on TV, with a scraggly beard and graying hair. If you looked at us together, we were truly an odd couple.

To my surprise, Dan didn't talk to me about Christianity, which I appreciated. Despite myself, I trusted him and sensed, from the first, that he was genuine.

In prison, I was free of Art Erickson, but Dan Taylor stepped in. He came regularly and, like Art, offered friendship and encouragement, constantly saying that he cared, and wanted the best for me.

By the time Dan had gotten to know me, he was able to talk to me straightforwardly and kept telling me that I could change. One time, he stared straight at me and said, "You're a bright young man, Johnny—smarter than most of the people in this prison. You need to go back to school."

I laughed; but I didn't forget.

———

By not getting into trouble at Stillwater, I was able to talk my way into minimum security. Two things pushed me to do that. First, I could have women visitors there, which meant sex. And second, as a loan shark, I could make more money since some of the inmates in minimum security were on work release.

One of the first things I did in minimum security was to recruit a big guy to work for me. He was a scumbag, exactly the kind of enforcer I needed.

Borrowers came to me because I was a nice guy (at least outwardly). Being tough has its limitations; being smart has none. I preferred using personality and persuasion, as opposed to violence. But some guys only responded to brute force.

I set up gambling games, and many of the work-release inmates got involved. After I cheated them out of their earnings, I'd loan them the money they lost. Of course, I made a nice profit. Even though the interest was exorbitant, in our culture, everyone understood how that worked. For me, it was a no-can-lose proposition.

Because I was fair in my business (despite my cheating), I made few enemies. When I loaned money, the borrower always knew what he had to pay me.

Another devious thing I did was I got some other guys to become lenders (with my money) and then charge too much. Then sometimes, I'd steer borrowers to them for a loan to pay me off. They never realized they were actually paying me twice.

Loan sharking was a safe way to make money. I refused to sell dope, which is far more dangerous. At least, I didn't have men sneaking up behind me, trying to hit me on the back of the head to steal my supply.

As despicable as it was, I learned how to make people hurt for defaulting on their loans from me. I used violence only as an absolute necessity, and always through others. Sometimes I made my guys hurt people who wanted to hurt me.

Another thing is that when I was on the street, I kept up my relationships with friends who were in prison. I was smart enough to realize that I might need them again one day. Since I made big money on the streets, I often sent my friends $500 or even $600 at a time. That's a lot of money in prison, but in case I was convicted, I wanted to have friends ready to stand up for me.

And that's exactly what happened.

When I received my sentence to Stillwater, I heard from some of my old friends. One of them sent me a letter, and the last line read, "Johnny, I've got your cell ready." That meant my friends would be looking out for me when I got there.

———

Although I still struggled with deep depression and frequent thoughts of suicide, Dan continued to visit every week. And that temporarily lifted my negative thoughts. Because he was my only visitor, I began to look forward to his coming. I never got into trouble again because I didn't want to lose the privilege of his visits.

Dan knew my past history of making trouble for the warden and being thrown "into the hole." But whenever the guard announced that Dan had come to see me, I proudly told the men in our cell block, "I'm going to see the professor." I wanted everyone to know that I was so smart a professor would come to see me.

But two things were important to me about Dan's visits. First, he cared about me. Second, he didn't have an agenda. He didn't want anything from me. We would sit and talk, mostly about educated things or ideas for various books for me to read. And I did read most of those he suggested—and enjoyed them.

His visits were the best part of every week. One day he sounded almost like Art, when he said, "Johnny, you're wasting your life."

No longer did I have to appear like the man who needed nothing. "You're right. I'm wasting my life. I want to change."

"Then go back to school." He said that at least once every time he visited. Over time, Dan convinced me that I truly was smart, but that I needed more formal education.

———

Dan's advice finally sank in and I did something strange to everyone. One day I went to the warden and said, "I want to go back to maximum security."

"Why would you want to do that?" he asked suspiciously. Inmates were constantly trying to con the guards and warden.

"I want to take college courses." Oddly enough, I could do that in maximum security but not in minimum.

After he questioned me for several minutes, he shrugged and said, "All right, you can go back."

Back in maximum security, I took some kind of test, and I scored very high. That meant I could choose what to study.

Dan had pushed me go to school, but he never told me what to study, even though I asked often.

"You have to figure it out," he always said. "Just think about it."

I did ponder the question. One thing about prison, it gives people a lot of hours to think.

At first I wanted to be a cosmetologist. But when I told that to Richard Grooves, the man in charge of education courses, he said, "The division of vocational rehabilitation won't pay for that."

"What do you mean?"

"You're too smart; plus you're a drug addict."

"What's that got to do with it?"

"That field is littered with drug dealers and addicts," he said. "We won't throw our money away on that. Besides, you'll lose interest after a while."

"No, I'm serious. When I get out of here, I'm going to go straight and I want to own a business."

"Then study something else—something that will benefit you for the rest of your life."

I was very Afro centric during that time, so I said with anger in my voice, "You white men like telling me, a black man, what I can't do. We hear that all the time. Since you have the keys to the money box, you're holding me hostage to your racist regime." I laid it on thick and swore a lot. But I couldn't touch him or I'd get in serious trouble.

He didn't respond.

After I calmed down, I asked, "Then what would *you* like me to go to school for, mister?"

"Computer programming."

"What? I don't even know what a computer is." Of course, I knew what they were. I'd seen people use them and stolen quite a few and sold them for a profit. But I didn't know anything about their inner workings, except how to steal the hard drives.

"Maybe not, but you can learn." He pointed to the results of my test score. "Everything here says you could easily learn computer skills. It's a growing field, so you'll only have more opportunities in the years ahead."

I shrugged. Why not? I thought, It can't hurt and I might learn some things.

In retrospect, that simple choice of studying computers would change the direction of my life.

18

LEARNING COMPUTERS

Two inmates taught the six-month course on computer programming: JP Morgan and Roy Wahlberg, both serving life sentences for murder. When it came to computers, they were geniuses. One of them, a lawyer, had written the first antivirus program.

To my surprise, I *was* a natural at computers. I easily grasped their lessons, which made me want to learn more. I was able to complete the six-month course in about two months.

One day, a guy in a suit came to the classroom during free time, where I was playing Scrabble with another inmate. I loved Scrabble and nobody ever beat me.

He looked at me and said, "Try spelling *omphaloskepsis*."*

My Scrabble opponent and everyone who was watching laughed and ignored him.

I thought about the word—which I'd never heard before. "Hm, *phala*. Ain't that navel or something?"

He smiled and said, "Try spelling that on your Scrabble game."

"That's too long." Then I said, "But spell it for me anyway."

As he spelled *omphaloskepsis,* I wrote it down. I don't why, but it was such a big word that it fascinated me.

He asked my name and we chatted for a couple of minutes. After he left, I turned to another inmate and asked, "Who was that?"

"That's Norburt Berg, the CEO of Control Data. He's the dude who sponsored the computer program."

---

* *Omphaloskepsis* literally means contemplation of the navel. It's a term used in meditation.

Surprisingly, I didn't forget the word. The man had impressed me and I remembered his name.

Shortly after that, I realized that I had acted stupidly when I got five years at my sentencing by insisting I hadn't committed the second crime. So I wrote to the judge, William F. Posten, and apologized for being stubborn. I also wrote that I had decided to return to school, and would complete the computer course soon. I added that I had served the two years he would originally have given me and I'd caused no problems. Then I asked him to review my case.

Everyone else laughed at me. "Won't do no good to send that letter."

"Man, he's black," someone else said, "and the toughest judge in the state of Minnesota."

"I don't care. I'm sending the letter."

Not long after that, Judge Posten subpoenaed me to court. When I stood before him, again, I apologized. "I shouldn't have acted that way." I told him what I had done in the computer course, about getting high grades, and finishing it in one-third of the time.

After he listened and thanked me for my change of attitude, he released me for the time I had served. "But you'll still be on parole for a year and a half."

"Thank you, sir," I said. "And I promise you won't regret it."

I am going to change.

At the time, I meant those words.

———

As soon as the guard brought me back to the prison, I handed him my release papers.

"You have to come inside and check out your things," he said.

"You keep everything in there. I'm not going back." I refused to walk back into the prison.

He let me walk away.

I was out of prison. I was a free man. My depression and suicidal thoughts were long gone. With my newly acquired skills I was going to make a different life for myself. I wouldn't mess up this time.

Within two weeks after my release, I messed up.

Back in Minneapolis, I went downtown dressed in a suit, looking for a job. I went to a temp agency to get something with computer programming, but nothing came of my efforts.

While I was still in the building, a nicely dressed African American left his office, but the door didn't close all the way. I snuck inside and realized it was the law office of John Jones. No one else was there, so I carefully searched and found a new credit card with the codes and names of all those who could use it.

At first, I had no problems using the card, but like most criminals, I made a mistake. I got high on drugs, went out in jeans instead of a suit, and stopped at a jewelry store to buy a $4,000 necklace.

The woman behind the counter sensed the card didn't belong to me. She excused herself momentarily and called the police.

They arrested me. And if that wasn't bad enough, I appeared before William F. Posten.

"I messed up," I said. "I couldn't find a job and didn't know what to do. I know it was wrong and I'm sorry. When I was walking by, a lawyer left the door open . . ." I told him exactly what happened.

"You were broke and you were looking for work, right?"

"I was." I told him I had tried a number of places and had just left the temp agency.

"There's something wrong with you," he said. Then he paused and stared at me.

To my surprise, he gave me probation on top of probation. Posten talked to my parole officer on the phone. "Don't violate Turnipseed. This man has potential and we're going to help make him successful."

If I had been a God-fearing man, I would have fallen to my knees and shouted praises. Instead I said, "Thank you, sir. You will not regret this."

Still nobody would hire me and I didn't want to go back to crime. Then I got an idea. I went to Control Data and asked to see Mr.

Berg. "My name is John Turnipseed," I told the receptionist. I was sure he would remember me because of my name.

She called Mr. Berg, who refused to take my call.

"Omphaloskepsis," I said. "Just tell him I said that word."

She started laughing. "You must know Norburt after all. He uses that word a lot." She called him back.

Mr. Berg asked her to give me the phone. "Where did you hear that word?"

"You told me in Stillwater Prison." I mentioned the Scrabble game.

He laughed. "I remember. You're the one who tried to figure out the word. How can I help you?"

"Sir, I took the class that you set up, passed the six months of lessons in two months. I'm out of prison now, but I can't find a job."

After a slight pause, he said, "Go to Control Data at Arden Hills." He gave me the name of the manager. "He'll take care of you."

I probably thanked him five times. As I drove out to the Minneapolis suburb, I thought, This is my chance. I *can* change. I can leave my past behind.

I had to.

———

The manager, whose name I no longer remember, was waiting for me when I arrived. He had me fill out information forms and gave me a job that day as a computer operator.

I can't explain it, and maybe it was because I was smart, but I caught on without effort. The work seemed simple. Within a short time I became the lead out of the eight computer operators.

Control Data had a super computer, which at that time, was one of only two fastest computers in the world. They trained me to use it.

How can I explain the contentment of knowing I was good at something that was honorable and good? I felt as if I had been made for that job and loved going to work.

The one problem I encountered was that Standard Oil of Ohio, our biggest customer, objected to me because of my criminal history. But because I was the best operator there, Control Data let me stay.

I came to work every day and worked hard and zealously. I had stopped getting high because of the work. For nearly two years I did fine, but then I got careless. I don't excuse myself because there is no excuse, but I started using drugs again. Drugs cost money and that led me back into a life of crime. My work performance went down and I lost my job. Seeing nowhere else to go, I went back to my old life of theft and burglary.

When I wasn't robbing, I was teaching several men how to burglarize buildings, and I'd fence the goods for them. I thought I was smart and I could do the masterminding. But I was still a criminal.

19

THE CRIMINAL PATTERN CONTINUES

My second son, Little Johnny, was born in 1973.

In 1990, at age seventeen, Little Johnny went to Glen Lake County Home. I visited him faithfully and brought him the kind of food he liked. I was proud of him and called him a chip off the old block.

Sometime later, Little Johnny was sent to the county home school in Red Wing. He was living the same way I had.

That's my son, I thought. I lived my life and thought it was good enough, so he felt it was all right to live the same way. But I didn't want my daughter, Lisa, to get into that kind of lifestyle.

Little Johnny was the toughest kid on the block and feared by almost everybody, even more than I had been. Several times my friends told me he'd robbed them, and they were scared of him.

Although I had been in and out of prison, my criminal life hadn't stopped. I never changed my criminal ways, not once.

All my sons sold dope along with me.

Good drugs make a lot of money because, when people run out of money, they bring merchandise—guns, jewelry, or anything that will sell. I'd buy and resell anything that produced a profit. Because they were desperate for another fix, they didn't bargain much.

Buying and reselling food stamps was another specialty. Everybody with whom I associated sold dope, and a number of addicts received food stamps.

For instance, one man had six kids and received $400 worth of food stamps each month. The addict would sell me the stamps at half-price, in this case $200. I resold them to a merchant for $300, and the merchant redeemed them for $400.

So the merchant and I each made $100, while the poor addict lost $200. The addicts took their kids to food shelves at places like the Methodist church. Because this was Minnesota, and the good people of the state weren't going to let kids starve.

I was making decent money with my various scams and drug deals. But I missed working with computers. And part of me still wanted to do something honest for a living.

Back when I first learned computer programming, I heard about a school called Resource Incorporated. During a visit there, I met a kid named Ricky, who was the son of an important black entrepreneur named Harry Davis.

Ricky was athletic and scholarly and didn't gravitate toward gangs and drugs. The tough kids hated him and made fun of his braces, but I liked him. Perhaps it was the memory of my own childhood. All I know is that I didn't like what I saw, so I became his protector.

He told his father what I had done for him, and Harry didn't forget.

I decided to ask Harry for a job. "In prison I was trained by two geniuses to be a computer operator, and I want to be a programmer."

"I'm sorry, John, but you don't have the skills for any of our current openings."

"I can do whatever you need," I insisted. "I know I can."

We talked for a time before he said, "I know you're a good kid but you've got a criminal history. It's going to be tough to get you a job."

We talked a little more. Then he said, "I tell you what, I have a friend who teaches a class at The Twin Cities Opportunities Industrial Center. But to get into his classes you have to pass the Computer Programmer Aptitude Battery."

"I'm willing to take the test."

It's a tough one," Harry said. "They've closed the interview process for the new class, but I'm sure I can get them to change their minds." He explained that the course was taught by IBM instructors, and all the students were black.

"It's top notch computer programming," Harry said.

"I'm ready for it."

Harry smiled, and added another hoop for me to jump through. "If they accept you, you have to be the top student in the class."

As I listened, I felt he didn't think I could make it, but that made me even more determined.

"I'll do that, and I'll be number one in class." I don't know if I was boasting or could really do it. I did know that I would give it everything I had. I had no idea what the Computer Programmer Aptitude Battery was, but I took the test anyway.

Afterward, the instructor said, "You blew the test out of the water. We'll take a chance on you because of Harry's recommendation."

I thanked him.

"You don't have the prerequisites, but your score makes me think you can do it."

I started with two disadvantages. First, as the man said, I didn't have the prerequisites and occasionally didn't know what they were talking about—but I asked questions or found out on my own. Second, I competed against people with four-year degrees. And of course, I had only a GED. It was a six-month course.

To my delighted surprise, the course the IBM people taught was almost the same as the one I had taken in prison. However, we were working on mainframes writing computer programs. That gave me a big advantage because I already knew how to do just about everything. I jumped ahead of the others and completed every assignment in two months—just as I had done in prison.

After I finished the final test, the teacher said, "We can't graduate you early because we're not set up for that. We have a job reserved for you—the top student. But we can't send you yet."

"So what do I do for the next four months?"

"Why don't you teach the lab course here?"

His words shocked me, but I didn't hesitate. "I'd like that."

I took the job, although I didn't get paid for it. I didn't care because I loved teaching the others. I helped other students—even those college graduates who were struggling. I didn't give them the answers, but I nudged them in the right direction.

More than once a student said, "Man, you rock. You should always teach this class."

"That's not what I want to do," I said. "I want to be a programmer."

When the time came for finals, I was helping two students debug a program. I looked up and saw a white woman walk into the classroom. I smiled at her.

"Excuse me, sir, but my name is Jane Larson. I'm hoping you can help me."

"What do you need help with?"

"I know almost nothing. I'm supposed to be a programmer, but I've never worked on this type of mainframe."

"Sure, I can help you with that."

I explained each piece of equipment, showed her how to log on and off, and spent most of the day with her. I wrote a few notes for her, and she thanked me profusely before she left.

The next morning, Jane came back. "I hate to bother you again, but will you give me just a little more help?"

"Sure," I said, and sat with her for about an hour and a half. She was a bright woman and caught on quickly.

Just before she left, Jane asked, "How would you like to work for me?"

"What do you mean *work for you*?"

"I'm starting a class at Resource Incorporated, and I need a teacher. You'd be a perfect fit."

"Ma'am, you don't know anything about me."

"What I know is what I felt when you taught me. You inspired me to know I could do it—and I did."

"But I already have a job waiting for me as soon as this course is over." I was so happy teaching I didn't want to leave.

"Working for whom?"

"The *Star and Tribune* newspaper."

"Oh, for Harry Davis? He's on our board, and he knows our school. I'll talk to him and try to convince him to pay your salary."

That's exactly what happened. I went to work for Resource Incorporated. I set up their computer equipment and showed Jane how to run six-month programs. At first, I taught every class.

Because Harry was holding my job as a computer programmer for the *Star and Tribune*, I taught her new lab instructor to take my place when the time came for me to leave. But I fell in love with teaching again and I didn't want to give up what I was doing. However, the newspaper would pay me almost double what Resource Incorporated offered.

I kept putting off starting my new job. Finally, the folks at the *Star and Tribune* put down an ultimatum: "If you're coming, you need to do it now."

I had to make a hard decision, so I talked it over with Jane.

"Get that practical experience for your career," she said. "You can always come back here."

"Really?"

"Certainly."

And I knew she meant it.

I went to the *Star and Tribune*. After three weeks, I received my first check. Each payday the other programmers went to cash their checks at a bar called Little Red Wagon, and they invited me to go with them. I wanted to fit in with these guys. They knew I had come in without a degree as a computer programmer and had also heard rumors about my background, including my time in prison. So I went with them.

By then, I could take or leave alcohol. One of them offered to buy me a drink, so I accepted a glass of wine. I was free of drugs—taking nothing in those days. I seemed to fit in with them, and they cheered me on. They kept inviting me to have more drinks.

I had a few more and I got drunk.

Then I realized if I was going to walk out of there on my own, I needed to leave right then. Down the street was a little bar called Cassius that catered to blacks. I walked over and saw all kinds of underworld people—they were easy for me to identify because they were the kind of people I had known most of my life.

I can't explain why, but I went inside and bought dope. That Friday night I ended up spending everything I had earned at the *Star and Tribune*. I ran out of money on Saturday and, still high, I decided to rob a business office.

I put on a suit, and went inside, around three o'clock in the morning. I found a cashbox full of money. As I was leaving the building, the glass door jammed. I had to break the glass to get out and that set off the alarm, but I got out of the building.

Several janitors must have heard the alarm going off and rushed to the front door to find out what had happened. They spotted the broken glass and me walking away.

"Excuse me, sir, do you know who broke the glass?" one of them yelled over the alarm. "Did you see anyone?"

I took off running. I had a cash box concealed under my suit and needed the money to get high again.

The janitors jumped in a car and chased me for three blocks until I was worn out. My mind wasn't clear enough to figure out how to elude them.

They grabbed me and held me until the police arrived. I pleaded guilty, and because it was a business burglary, they only gave me two years.

My third prison sentence.

After my release from prison, I didn't have a job and couldn't find one. I didn't want to try the *Star and Tribune because* they wouldn't even talk to me.

I went to Resource Incorporated to pick up my resume.

"Why do you need your resume?" Jane Larson asked. "What happened to you?"

"You don't know?"

She shook her head, so I told her—everything. She listened while I talked. After I finished, she said quietly, "Why don't you come back to work for us?"

"Doing what?"

"Teaching, John, what else? I've been holding down the fort," she said. "My last assistant is leaving, and I need a good teacher. If you take the job, I think I can get you licensed."

"Even knowing about my messing up, you still want me?"

"I don't care about your past. I know you're a good man, and you were kind to me. You inspired me when I didn't know anything about computers. So yes, I want you."

Jane was as good as her word. She opened the door for me and I went back to work for Resource Incorporated. I started as lab instructor, moved up to assistant teacher, then to teacher, and finally to manager.

Jane was given the opportunity to become the director for disabled students at a community college. Because I didn't have a degree, I couldn't replace her, so Resource Incorporated hired John Wagner, who became my boss.

I hadn't been gambling while I was teaching there. But suddenly, without knowing why, I started again and the old addiction kicked in. So in order to support my habit, I started stealing again. Eventually I had a total of ten felonies, and I don't remember which one got me back before a judge. Although I never used a gun again because that would have been armed robbery, and I wasn't violent.

I came before a judge—a different one. He took pity on me. From my record, he saw that I had once been violent, but wasn't any longer.

Again a miracle happened. He dropped the charges.

Neither the judge nor the police knew that my gang involvement had picked up. I was heading back to my old ways again.

20

THE SHOOTING OF LITTLE JOHNNY

In 1992, while in jail for theft—I was in and out of jail a lot—I received a phone call in the middle of the night. Little Johnny had been shot.

I felt like I'd taken a bullet to the chest myself. But considering the way I lived, it wasn't all that surprising.

As I understand, it happened this way. When the Turnipseed family had parties, it was the way some of the Mafia movies portray gangs. Everybody checked their guns at the door because there was alcohol served and most of them had learned that guns and alcohol don't mix.

To enforce the no-guns-inside rule, the family hired two armed men to stand outside. Two more men on bicycles rode up and down the streets and alleys patrolling the outer perimeter. Every fifteen minutes the bikers checked with the two on the door.

Two additional men sat in cars or vans before the party and until after it was over. The police might drive by, but because of highly tinted windows they couldn't see the men sitting inside. But then, neither could other gangbangers.

Whoever ran the party told Johnny to leave because he was drunk and upsetting people. He wasn't well liked by most of the family members as he had violated too many rules. Many considered him a spoiled bully, but because of me—my protection—no one could do anything to him.

When Little Johnny left, the guard at the door wouldn't give him back his gun. "You're drunk," the man said. "We'll hand it back after you sober up."

"Okay," Little Johnny said, and left.

He had parked his car about a block away. That was standard because we didn't want the police to see a lot of cars near one house. Otherwise they might call in the numbers of the license plates and figure out it was a Bloods gang meeting.

A guard on a bicycle rode in front of Little Johnny, escorting him to his car. That much seems clear. When my son turned the corner, the rider disappeared. Just then, four men came out from behind the bushes and opened fire, point blank.

When I heard about the incident, I raised two questions (and they were never answered): How did they know Little Johnny would be there? What happened to the guard on the bicycle?

In our entire Bloods history, no one had ever been shot while he was with an armed escort. A few times, someone had been shot at from a distance, but never at close range. Wasn't it strange that with two men on bicycles and two men in parked cars nearby that none of them could prevent the shooting?

For that to happen to Little Johnny had to be a conspiracy within the Bloods—again, something that hadn't happened before. When the Bloods had parties, everyone knew the people were heavily protected. And yet even with all the protection, four men ambushed and shot Little Johnny.

———————

Little Johnny was hit thirteen times, and they shot off his right leg with the first blast and half of his left leg with the second. One shooter emptied his gun in Little Johnny's chest. The only reason my son didn't get shot in the face was because he put up his hand and the bullet shattered his wrist.

"He probably won't make it through the night," the surgeon told the family.

Little Johnny didn't die, which was a miracle.

As a result, my son became an urban legend like the famous gangster Legs Diamond. The message came across loud and clear, "I'm tough. You can't kill me."

No one doubted that the shooting had been gang-related and, most obviously done by members of the Bloods. I have no doubts about it because Little Johnny had violated the strong family code by robbing the wrong person, cheating another, and shooting a third—all of them people he should have left alone. But the worst crime was that Little Johnny's best friend had killed a member of the Turnipseed family. Killing a family member was at the top of the list of things the Bloods didn't do. After that, most of the family turned against him.

Shooting Little Johnny also benefited rival gangs. Not only had he been one of the founding members, but he was also one of the chief enforcers of the Bloods, so many people wanted to kill him.

Because of that incident, Little Johnny formed a new gang. He was joined by my stepson, Roamel, whom the Bloods didn't like. Because I adopted him into the family, some of them refused to accept him as a real Turnipseed.

Little Johnny called their new gang CAN, also all African American and involved in murders, robberies, and drug dealing. Copying the Crips in Los Angeles, they wore blue to distinguish themselves from the Bloods who still wore the baseball caps with a red B. From then on, like the Hatfields and McCoys, the two gangs became natural enemies.

With the CAN's protection, Little Johnny could walk the streets, safe from the Bloods who still wanted to kill him. Although he didn't do much walking. He was too tough to get an artificial leg, so he has used crutches ever since.

Despite the intervention of Art Erickson, Father Capoochi, and Dan Taylor, I remained hardened. But I started crying, and couldn't seem to stop. The last dope I had used came from one of my sons, who sold it to me. That was my legacy: My son sold dope, so did my stepson, and my cousin. I went down the line and ticked off name after name. I could get a $1,000 worth of dope just on my word, whether I paid it back or not. Sometimes I did, sometimes I didn't.

But when I almost lost my son, who was following my footsteps, I knew I had to change.

That night I quit smoking dope; I've never touched it again.

I will change. I have to change.

Then I remembered something from my days at Stillwater Prison. One of my friends there told me about Urban Ventures in Minneapolis. That didn't mean anything to me, but he said they truly wanted to rehabilitate people, and to make them useful members of society.*

I don't recall anything more because that conversation had taken place seven or eight years earlier. I thought about it.

Was it too late?

I had to try. I was broken. I felt I had lost everything of value in life. Not only had I ruined my own life, I had broken so many others. I was nothing but a thug, a criminal. I wasn't gangbanging, and I no longer had any taste for violence.

I cried all night, even after I heard that Johnny would survive.

And for the first time in more than forty years, I prayed. "God, forgive me," I begged. "Give me another chance. Please, help me."

———

In 1994, in a plea bargain to get out of going to prison again, I agreed to go to Eden House for nine months to a year. Their policy stated that *they provided recovery, accountability, and support services to facilitate individuals and families to move from nonproductive behavior to responsible, self-sufficient lifestyles.*

While there, I heard that Urban Ventures was sponsoring a new program called the Center for Fathering.

"What's that?" I asked at Eden House.

"They help you connect with your kids and teach you how to be a real father."

"That so?"

"And they do things like teach you how to apologize, or do whatever you need to do to be a better dad."

---

* Urban Ventures programs focus on job development, education, and families. A major goal is to break the cycle of generational poverty in South Minneapolis.

I liked that, and even though I didn't know if they could help me, I asked for permission to go to the Center for Fathering. They approved my going for the weekly group meetings.

To my surprise, I learned that Art Erickson had left his job at the Methodist church and was working at the Center for Fathering. I smiled to think about it. Art had started working on me when I was a teenager. I was finally caving in.

Not only was Art there, but I learned that he was the person who started the Center for Fathering. I never doubted that he would help me. He accepted me—as he always had. Even so, I was ashamed.

We sat in a conference room and I told him everything. Before we left, Art and I decided to meet on a regular basis.

Art said, "We're all sinners and will sin the rest of our lives." Then he said something I would hear several times: "Pain will lead you to God, and success will lead you away."

I became their first client in the new program. They were willing to help me try to figure out my life. I was changing, but how could I convince my kids? I wanted to be a real parent to them. I didn't miss a single meeting at the Center.

After I finished my nine months at Eden House, I was licensed by the State of Minnesota, as a teacher, qualified to teach an accredited course on computer programming at a school for physically disabled adults.

I wanted to change my behavior, but inside I was still the same. Though I didn't go back to drugs, I got involved in crime again—usually having someone else do the jobs while I worked behind the scenes.

I just couldn't see how to escape my old career.

John as 4 year old in Selma, Alabama, 1958.

John and his brothers. John is the oldest on the right, and then counter clockwise is Isaiah, Sterling, Jerome, and Michael (bottom center).

John behind bars at St. Cloud State Reformatory in 1975.

John as a pimp in the late 70s.

John's son Shaun Ramon Eason who was murdered.

John's children left to right - Lisa, Dee, and Johnny Edwards.

John as a teacher.

Childhood friend Joe Edwards with his wife Florabell and family.

John and son Little Johnny on crutches the night at the bonfire event.

John with Turnipseed family members. From left to right are Dee, Duncan, Michael, Darryl, John, Otis, and Jerome. Markalow is the youngest front and center.

John with his mom Earlene.

John (center) with sons Dee (left) and Tyray.

John's wife Teresa.

On the set of Turnipseed Legacy, the third short film about John's story. Left to right:
John, producer James Duke, mentor Art Erickson, actor Lawrence Gilliar, Jr., and director Joby Harris.

On the set of *Turnipseed Legacy*.

James Duke on the left, the director of the Turnipseed film. Art Erickson on right,
former CEO of Urban Ventures and John's mentor.

John's sister Bonita.

Left to right: grandson Lionell, daughter Lisa, Sharon Edwards, and daughter Jamie.

John (right) with sons Johnny Edwards (left) and Tyray Perry (center).

21

CAUGHT

I had been so evil, I couldn't have gone to face Art. That didn't matter; Art came to me. He was always available if I needed him. Even though I felt guilty all the time and, deep down, knew turning to God was the answer, I wasn't ready.

One time, Art told me, "I will defend you, so you'll never have to defend yourself. And you defend me, so I'll never have to defend myself."

That sounded like gang stuff. It didn't make a lot of sense, but I didn't forget. Later, I realized how seriously Art meant those words. A time would come when I couldn't defend myself, and Art was there.

I trusted Art because he laid the tracks years earlier by consistently helping me and attempting to build a relationship with me, even when I wanted nothing to do with him.

The other person I thought might be able to help me, besides Art, was my mother. I went to see her and told her what a terrible son I'd been (as if she didn't know).

She listened, hugged me, kissed my cheek, and said, "It'll be all right, baby."

I expected nothing less from my mom, who never gave up on me. But as much as I appreciated her consistent unconditional love, she couldn't answer the question that tormented me constantly: *Why can't I be a good man?*

My life was a mess. I was more than forty years old, a terrible person, and didn't deserve to live. I wanted to be good, but I couldn't change.

I felt hopeless.

The police constantly watched me, so I couldn't pull any burglaries. But I could send out others.

In addition to masterminding crimes, I could play the decoy. While the police followed me to one place, my gang was robbing in another area.

But even as my crime sprees continued, deep inside I knew they would catch me eventually.

Even when a doctor told me I had to have a hernia repaired, that didn't stop my criminal activities. I set up a number of places for my gang to hit while I was in the hospital. By the time I came home, they had run out of places I'd scheduled for them to rob.

After I recovered from surgery, I went back to gambling. Even though I had gotten away from the habit, it always came back. "I can handle it," I'd tell myself. But before long, the occasional game turned into a full-blown addiction. I often lost $10,000 or more in a single night.

I had to go back to doing robberies myself to make up for all my losses.

During the daytime I staked out potential places. I'd go into a business office or a jewelry store. While casually walking around looking at merchandise, I checked out their alarm system and took note of how they had set up their security guards. How many computers did they have? Where was the safe? It was also very important to find a way in and out of the place.

On a Friday evening, I'd go to the office or store alone, dressed like a prosperous businessman. I waited until the employees were leaving for the day, then walked in the door as someone was coming out. I walked quickly as if I were late for an important meeting. Often the departing employee would hold the door open and say, "Hey, come on in."

Once inside, I went to the office where the safe was kept and peeked through the door. If it was empty, I could take my time. If someone was in there, I stepped into the sanitation supply closet and slipped on my janitor's uniform, which I always brought with me, over my suit. Then I grabbed some cleaning equipment and walked into the office.

"Could you leave for a minute?" I'd ask. "I'm running behind and I need to get this done right away."

No one ever questioned me. They always left.

After disabling the alarm, I broke into the safe and took the money. On Saturday morning, my gang would go in and take all the computers and anything else we could sell. Most of the time, the police didn't realize there'd been two different burglaries.

When I went in on my own, I took only money. But after a company was hit, they didn't expect a second robbery. So that's exactly what I did. I didn't realize it at the time, but by hitting them twice, I was establishing a pattern. Eventually, the police figured it out.

———

One day, as I walked out of my apartment building, I saw a tall white man in a suit standing in the parking lot. He glared at me in a way that made me feel funny. I stared back thinking, *He must hate black guys.*

Three times that week, I saw the same man in different locations.

When I was staking out the next place to rob, I kept hearing footsteps in the otherwise silent building. And the elevator stopped at every single floor.

As a precaution, I took the stairs when I was ready to leave. As I was walking out of the building with the money, I saw that same tall white man coming toward the door. I hurried away before he saw me.

A few days later, I cased a building in Edina, the richest suburb in Minneapolis. At closing time, just before I went inside, a car drove by very slowly. The driver was that same man.

I rebuked myself, "Get over it. You're just paranoid. That dude isn't following you."

I went inside and walked toward the main office. In the hallway I spotted that same white man coming my way. My heart raced. But he ignored me and kept walking.

Man, I really am paranoid.

After he passed me, I went inside an office. One of the first things I found was $2,000 worth of postage stamps. "I'll take these," I whispered to myself. I knew a man who would buy them for half their retail price.

Then I spotted a new Coach briefcase, beautiful and professional looking. Impulsively, I decided to take it with me. Inside I found $400 cash and the receipt for it, listing the price as $1,000.

I put the stamps inside the briefcase along with $2,000 cash I found in the safe.

I left, holding the Coach briefcase. In my previous robberies, I always stuffed everything inside my coat pockets so I wasn't carrying anything in my hands. I knew it was stupid, but I was too focused on the big haul I'd just made.

As I started down the hallway, two white men came walking in my direction. One of them was the man I'd seen before. I looked at them both with confidence and kept walking.

As the tall man came close, he said, "Hi, Johnny,"

So I wasn't paranoid after all. This dude really had been following me. He knew who I was, and was aware that my family was a "criminal enterprise."

The two detectives arrested me. They had seen me go inside empty-handed and now I carried a briefcase. There was no escape from this; they had me. They took me and the briefcase full of stolen goods to the police station.

Since the detective had followed me to several places I'd robbed, I expected to be charged with multiple robberies. But they only arrested me for this one.

I'd lost count of the number of times I'd been arrested and thought I'd gotten off easy this time. But something unexpected happened that would change my life.

22

THE CONFESSION

I was a pro at talking to the police. Ever since they caught me through my thumbprint, I had learned to never give away anything, and stay tight-lipped. I even felt a little smug. But this time I'd been caught with the evidence.

For some reason, as soon as the questioning began, I broke down and began weeping. Convulsively.

What's wrong with me?

The detective waited patiently for me to stop, but I couldn't. Just when I'd think I was through, the tears would flow again.

"Would you like some water?" he asked.

I couldn't speak, but may have nodded. The detective left the interview room and came back with a glass of water, napkins, and a tape recorder. He pushed the water and napkins toward me, sat down, started the tape, and waited.

When I finally stopped crying, he asked in a quiet voice, "You got anything you want to say?"

"Yeah, man. I've been stealing. I've also got a gambling problem. And I'm really tired of this kind of life."

"We can help each other."

I'd heard that one before. "How?"

"We have between forty and sixty burglaries in Edina that we think you did. If you confess to all of them, I'll speak up for you with your probation officer."

Because I was on probation, I would not be able to get bail. So without hesitating, I said, "Okay." I didn't care. I had to change. Even if it meant spending the rest of my life in prison, the peace of mind would be worth it.

The detective went down the list of dates and places, and I confessed to every one of the burglaries.

They knew me better than I imagined. But that was only the beginning. They then contacted the other five precincts I'd committed crimes in. All together, I confessed to more than fifty crimes, but the detective rounded them down and charged me with only fifty.

Because I had been caught in Edina, I made a deal only with the police there. That made the other precincts angry. They wanted the Edina police to send me to their cities.

To my surprise, the detective refused. "No sense in shipping John and having him plead guilty to more charges. Not only would it not be to his advantage, but we have enough here to keep him inside for a long, long time."

No one could force me to go to the other precincts. They didn't have the evidence to convict me.

"Just tell us the names of your crew (a term I never used), John, and it will go easier on you," the detective said.

"I don't know what you're talking about."

"Okay." He shrugged, and I realized he hadn't expected me to give up my friends, but he had to try.

While I was in jail awaiting trial, Art Erickson came to see me. He stuck by me and attended every court hearing. I can't think of a time when he didn't come through for me, regardless of what I needed, anything from cash to advice. All my old so-called friends had disappeared.

With Art's help, I struck a deal with the detective. "If you'll let me finish teaching my computer class," I said, "I'll plead guilty." The class still had nine months to go.

The judge granted me one year to "set your affairs in order" before my sentencing. My sentence would be a minimum of ten years and could be as long as twenty.

During that year of freedom I wanted to soak in everything I could by going to the meetings at the Center for Fathering. I still had sixteen weeks to go to finish my fathering class.

The detective called Ann Geige, my parole officer. "We have John Turnipseed here, and he's going to help us. In return, we're letting him out on bail. But we'd like you to keep him out of jail."

Ann agreed.

As a provision of postponing my sentence, I had to post a $30,000 bail and live by strict rules.

My daughter Lisa helped me out by paying for the lawyer. And I put up my house to get the money for bail. But that didn't bother me. It's only money, I told myself. Although an expensive arrangement, I was more concerned about not spending the time in jail than what it cost me to stay out. I could always come up with cash.

Even worse and more shameful, my family thought I was doing better. They truly believed I had reformed. Lisa was proud of her daddy. At one time I'd impulsively promised, "I'll never go back to prison." I meant those words when I said them.

Then I went back to prison, and it had almost destroyed her. I hated telling her I was now facing prison again—this time with a long, long sentence.

———

Because of my financial situation, I went back to gambling.

I went to a casino almost every day. The most I took (and lost) in one day was $20,000. The bosses liked seeing me come in because I always had cash.

I especially liked playing blackjack, poker, and electronic craps. If I won the first time I bet, I'd bet double or nothing the next time. Crazy I know, but I doubled each bet I won, so after three or four times I was broke.

But I didn't care because I could easily replenish my losses. If I ran out of money I'd stolen, I could always tap a few guys who owed me.

But an addiction takes precedence over everything else in life. One time when I ran out of money, I hurried back to my apartment and got out a box that I always threw my change into. I counted out nearly $4,000. Throwing the coins back inside, I took the box back to the casino and continued to play—until I lost it too.

Art and I had developed a relationship. And I finally told him about my addiction.

"Why didn't you tell me before?"

"I didn't want you to know. Besides, I'm not used to this being honest thing. In fact, I can't even explain why I'm telling you now."

Art listened, then urged me to talk to my parole officer, Ann Geige. I set up an appointment with her for that same afternoon.

"So," she said as she closed her office door, "you're back on drugs, are you?"

"No, not drugs," I said, too ashamed to look at her. "Gambling."

I could tell from the expression on her face that she didn't believe me.

"I have a credit line of ten thousand dollars at four gambling casinos. Just call any of them and mention my name. They'll tell you."

She called Mr. Glake at one of the casinos and asked him about John Turnipseed.

"Yes, I know John. He's an excellent customer. Never any problems with him. Is he in any trouble?"

"Just checking on him," she said.

Then she turned to me. "Well, I'm glad it's not drugs again, but you need to get help with your gambling."

"Yes, ma'am," I said, but I didn't do anything about it.

I went back to teaching computer programming to physically disabled adults as if nothing had happened. No one at school knew I was on parole. I concentrated on finishing the class, knowing I'd be going to jail immediately after.

23

NO LONGER ALONE

Three days after my arrest, a student ran into the room in the middle of class. "Sorry to interrupt, but there's a TV reporter here. He's got a camera crew and everything. And wants to talk to you, Mr. Turnipseed." He grinned, probably assuming the reporter was going to publicize the wonderful work I was doing at the school.

But I knew why they were there. "I—I need a break," I said.

Using the back entrance, I went out to the parking lot and lit up a cigarette. As I was smoking, one of the men I'd met at the drug treatment center walked by. When he saw me, he started telling me how great he thought I was because I had sobered up. "God said there will be storms coming, and if you just believe in Him, that storm will pass." He smiled and walked on.

He's crazy, I thought.

After I finished my cigarette, I headed back toward the classroom. The TV people were outside my office door, and my students had gathered around, wondering what was happening. I brushed past everyone without a word, went into my office, and locked the door.

I was miserable and couldn't face anyone, especially my students. They didn't know I had a criminal history. And I'd let Jane Larson down because she had helped me get my teaching license from the State of Minnesota. If the truth about me got out, it would embarrass me and everyone who cared about me. It would also hurt people who didn't deserve to be hurt.

I wanted to run away, but I couldn't do that to my family, and I would eventually have to face things like a man. Even if I could, where would I go?

The noise outside my office grew louder. Someone knocked hard. Instead of answering, I pushed a heavy metal cabinet against the door. I wedged everything I could find against that door so no one could break in.

"John," someone said, "they want to see you."

"Go away."

A few times someone tried to force the door open. After a while, they gave up.

I collapsed onto the cement floor in a corner of the room and started crying. I bawled so hard my stomach hurt. I writhed on the floor, trying to hold back the sobs.

Finally, I got up. My black suit was now chalky white, but I didn't care. I grabbed the phone to call my mother, but I accidentally called Lisa. "I'm going to embarrass you again. I just wanted you to know. I'm sorry . . ." The tears flowed so hard I couldn't finish.

"Just give it to Jesus." Thanks to my mom, Lisa had grown up in the church and she was a believer.

After I hung up, her words kept ringing through my mind: "Just give it to Jesus."

"Jesus, take me," I moaned. "I'm no good and I'm not worth saving. But please, please accept me."

For several minutes I pleaded with Jesus Christ to change my life. Then, in a flash, my tears stopped flowing. A deep sense of peace came over me. I'd never experienced anything like this in my entire life. Though I couldn't explain it, I knew Jesus Christ had accepted me. I didn't know what was going to happen, but I knew it would be all right.

I dusted off my suit the best I could. Then I asked God for two things. "Please, God, let my kids forgive me, and let me keep teaching."

In that moment, I felt assured that God would enable my kids to forgive me.

As I moved toward the door, I said, "God, I can't do this on my own. I need You. You have to take over." The deep peace was so strong I felt like I had five thousand soldiers with rifles protecting me. Nothing bad could happen to me.

I pulled everything away from the door, and opened it. The reporter and his crew had gone, but my students stood there, gaping at me.

"You okay?" someone asked.

I smiled, even though my cheeks were stained with tears. "I'm fine."

They must have thought I'd lost my mind, or that I was high on drugs. I couldn't put my experience into words, but I knew—with a certainty I'd never had before—I was going to be all right.

As I walked out of the office, my boss came up to me. "What happened?"

"I can't talk right now. Can I go home?"

"Yes, of course."

I went directly to see Art. Tears flowed again as I told him everything. Finally I said, "I don't know much about this Jesus thing, but I have surrendered to Him. I don't know what's next. Am I supposed to do something?"

"No. But I'd like us to meet regularly so we can pray together." Art prayed for me right then.

Our true, deep relationship began that day.

———

A TV reporter named Tom Lyden, from local channel 9, did a report on me during the nine o'clock evening news. First, he presented the good things about me: that I had reformed (which I really hadn't), that I taught my class, showed up on time, and did a fine job, and that my students were devoted to me. Then he exposed me as he told about my crimes. He accused me of being the leader of a gang of thieves. Since I was, I couldn't dispute that.

Mr. Turnipseed was now Mr. Criminal on TV and everyone would know the truth. That thought crushed me. The news feature forced me to see myself for what I was. And I despised what I saw.

———

I went to the Eden House treatment center and spoke with the director of their after-care group. They considered me a star because of the changes I'd made since I finished my time there a year or so earlier.

I told the director about the fifty felonies I'd confessed to. As a result, Eden House disowned me, claiming I had humiliated them. And they were right to do that. I had violated my agreement with them. I felt desperate. And alone.

But faithful Art remained in my life. He listened to me talk. He didn't always answer right away. He liked to think about things first. If I asked him something, he might not give me the answer for two days. That was all right. After all, I had ruined my life. What could anyone do for me?

I didn't ask Art to intervene in my upcoming sentencing. But after that TV program aired, Art took me to meet with the judge and asked him to extend my parole. "He's finished the classes on fathering and he's been our best student. If you extend his parole, I'll hire him to teach a parenting class."

The judge knew Art, as did almost everyone in law enforcement. And they trusted him because of the years he had lived in the community. They knew he was committed to lifting up lost and hopeless people—like me.

To my surprise, the judge agreed.

As pleased as I was, I didn't know why, and I didn't ask. It was grace, but I hadn't yet added that word to my every day living vocabulary.

After the news sank in, I told Art, "I don't have the qualifications to teach at the Center."

"You can do it," Art said matter-of-factly. He saw something in me that I didn't. He believed in me when I couldn't believe in myself.

24

THE SENTENCE

I taught the remainder of the school year, and when I finished, I was ready for my sentencing. The peace God had given me didn't leave. I didn't know what lay ahead of me, but I knew it couldn't be as awful as what lay behind me.

I later learned that Art had written letters and gotten support for me from the former governor of Minnesota, Al Quie.

I also learned that the career criminal division, which only goes after serious crimes, was going to prosecute me. They hated me and my family and everything we stood for. And who could blame them? I represented the Rolling 30s Blood Street Gang, who were arch criminals. I was sure the judge would want me put away for as long as possible.

I didn't tell them I had become a Christian. Just about every career criminal "finds Jesus" when they get caught, even Muslims. For most, it doesn't last. But I didn't want to wave a Jesus flag and then fail two months later.

The Sunday before I went to court, I attended Speak the Word Church. Right in the middle of his sermon, Pastor Randy Morrison said, "Somebody in here is hurting."

The words didn't grab me until he added, "Somebody in here is experiencing accusations against him, but he's a different person now. And God knows that."

I was shocked. *He is speaking to me.*

"Whoever you are, I want you to know that God is your judge and Jesus is your lawyer."

I broke down crying. When the pastor gave an altar call, I rushed forward and fell on my knees. I'd already given my life to Christ, but those words broke me and I knew I needed prayer. A couple of people prayed for me and I left in peace.

I had no idea what would happen. But Jesus was my lawyer, and that was enough.

Less than a week before the sentencing, my wife and I went to the courtroom to meet with the judge. We sat quietly in the back row and watched the judge's court administrator, a white woman in her late twenties, get things ready.

When my lawyer walked into the courtroom, the administrator called out, "Hey, Jerry. How you doing?"

"I'm good." He smiled and walked up to her.

"What are you here for?"

"I'm here to try to seal the deal for John Turnipseed."

"John Turnipseed? Not a chance. I've read his file. You know he's dirt, don't you?" She went on and on about how bad I was and what I deserved. "We're going to lock him up for as long as we can."

My wife started crying. The administrator looked at us, but clearly didn't recognize me. Because I was nicely dressed, I'm sure she thought I was a lawyer and the woman was my client.

My lawyer pointed to me. "That's John back there."

She looked extremely embarrassed. "Oh. I'm sorry."

Just then, the judge walked in. My lawyer told him how hard I'd been working and that I had completed the course at the Center for Fathering.

To my surprise, the judge made a verbal deal to reduce my sentence from ten years to eighty-five months.

I silently thanked God. I hadn't expected the judge to cut any amount of time from my sentence—certainly not almost three years. I was a three-time loser, so this was a huge break.

I had to return to court later for my official sentencing. I told Art, "There's no need for you to come. I'll keep in touch."

"Are you sure?"

"I don't want anyone there. I've been a criminal all my life. Now it's time to pay for my sins and to show everyone the change the Lord has made in me."

"If that's what you want, all right," Art said. "I'm still going to pray."

"Okay. Please pray that God will make me faithful while I'm in prison and that I'll never go back to my old ways."

———

Except for my lawyer, I went to court alone. I arrived a little early for the sentencing, perhaps because of my anxiety, and stood at the door, waiting for the bailiff to open the courtroom.

Two of my cousins sat on a nearby bench, both members of my old gang. That didn't surprise me. The word had spread that I would receive seven years for committing fifty felonies. Even though I insisted to everyone that I had done nothing to get a lighter sentence, the Bloods wanted to find out for themselves whether I'd snitched on someone in the gang.

Though the judge had verbally agreed to make this deal, he had to declare it officially during the sentencing. So my family had checked the public records to find out when I was scheduled for court and sent a couple of representatives.

———

My lawyer called and told me that the prosecutor in my case (who was not a Christian, and had only reluctantly agreed to the shorter sentence) had a scheduling conflict. Normally when that happens, the judge postpones court for about a week. However, for some reason, the judge agreed to let an assistant district attorney fill in.

When the new ADA arrived, he started chatting with me about the weather and sports. I realized that he thought I was another lawyer. I didn't correct him.

"We're going to lock up a very bad man today," he said.

I didn't say anything.

He checked his watch. "I need to get done with this Turnipseed case. Is he your client?"

"No, that's me."

"*You're* Johnny Turnipseed?"

"Yes."

He quickly opened his file and checked my mug shot. "Oh, man, I'm sorry."

I shrugged, not having any idea what to say. After all, he was right; I was a very bad man.

He stared at my mug shot, scratching his head. "Something's wrong with this. I don't want to lock you up."

His words shocked me. He wasn't even supposed to be talking to me, much less giving me his opinion.

Before he could say anything more, the courtroom door opened and we went inside. My lawyer rushed into the courtroom and directed me to the defense table.

Whatever happens today, Lord, it's all in Your hands.

When it came time for me to plea, I answered one word: "Guilty."

My lawyer asked for leniency and said, "I appeal to the mercy of the court."

When the judge, Gary Larson, called for the prosecutor's response, he said simply, "We ask for leniency."

Tears filled my eyes. I could hardly believe those words.

My parole officer, Ann Geige, testified for several minutes. In essence, she said, "Scientists have proven that if people are forty years old or thereabouts, they're more likely to change their lives."

I don't know where she got that data, and it sounded like some theory someone made up. But I wasn't going to argue.

"Your honor," she said, "I will work with Mr. Turnipseed if you give him probation." She made a compassionate plea for me not to go to prison, affirming that I had changed.

That was a gutsy thing for Ann to do because she put her reputation on the line. (Later I found out that she had postponed her retirement to be there for my sentencing.) But I still didn't think the judge would agree to any additional leniency, let alone parole.

In one sense, it didn't matter. Ann believed in me. So did Art. And others were beginning to trust me. I knew I'd never forget their kindness.

The prosecutor looked at my lawyer and asked, "How about two consecutive years in the workhouse to satisfy the police?"

I couldn't believe what I had heard. If Judge Larson agreed, I could teach my class during the day and come back to the workhouse at night.

But I knew the police wouldn't be satisfied with that arrangement. They had worked hard to catch me and they certainly didn't want to let me go. To them, two years in the workhouse would be like setting me free.

Judge Larson stared at both attorneys, then at me, and then looked down at his papers. After several seconds he stared at me again. "Mr. Turnipseed, there's definitely something different about you."

Ann looked as if she were ready to cry. She had been my parole officer for years, and she had seen something different in me too. She knew me and had "violated me." That is, because I violated my parole, she sent me back to prison.

"So be it," the judge said. "Two consecutive years in the workhouse." He leaned forward and pointed his gavel at me. "I'm jumping out on a limb for you. If you ever come back here, even for something minor, I'm going to bury you."

"I won't, sir. I promise you. And thank you, your honor. You will never be sorry."

The police officers in the courtroom couldn't say anything, but their angry faces clearly showed they had hoped to get rid of me until I was sixty or older.

My two gang-member cousins looked more confused than anyone. They had come to see me receive a sentence of at least seven years, and instead, I was able to walk out of the courtroom. Despite their shock, they realized I hadn't cut a deal with the judge, and that satisfied the family.

I wasn't even taken into custody, which was another act of God's grace. Judge Larson gave me a week to get my affairs in order before I had to report to the workhouse. He also said I could have a once-a-week furlough to go to Urban Ventures and visit Art Erickson.

That was absolutely wonderful. And crazy.

I could hardly take in what had happened. Why had God been so forgiving? How had the Lord changed the hearts of the court officials?

(I didn't know it then, but not only was Ann a Christian, so was Judge Larson, and the substitute ADA.)

Just then, I remembered the words spoken to me by the man I'd met in the treatment center.

"And God said there will be storms coming, and if you just believe in Him, that storm will pass."

My storm had passed. And now I understood grace.

25

THE WORKHOUSE AND MARRIAGE

No one at the workhouse could believe what had happened to me. Repeatedly, people asked, "How did you do it?"

I didn't know much about God or the Bible, but in my simple way, I told them that God's first miracle in my life was saving me. I told them about Art Erickson and the Center for Fathering.

"Who is this guy?" they asked. "How do I get to go see him?"

———

As part of my two-year workhouse sentence, the community college where I had taught subcontracted me to teach computer programming at Resource Incorporated. My students were severely disabled adults who, for various reasons, couldn't adapt to the normal workplace.

I loved the work and the challenge. One day, in the middle of a class, a man needed his catheter changed. I gladly did it, thankful to God for an opportunity to help other people.

I researched all the latest computer programs and figured out how to use or modify them for my students. For those who couldn't use their hands well, I modified the equipment so they could use a software program called Dragon Dictate, which had just been developed, where the computer typed as they spoke. I loved my students. I enjoyed teaching them, and I wanted them to succeed.

A grant allowed severely disabled adults to receive college credit if they attended classes for eight hours a day, five days a week. If they stayed with the program for nine months, they received thirty-five college credits.

I required all of my students to pass the Computer Programmer Aptitude Battery that many people failed.

Despite their disabilities, I was strict with them. They could be late only one time a month. I wanted them to get jobs as computer programmers and my reports would show their faithful attendance. Part of my job was to line up employers to take my graduating students. "But if you can't adhere to this rigorous program," I challenged them, "I'm not going to help get you a job." I didn't want to encourage employers to hire my students merely out of sympathy.

My students responded well to this. They all worked extremely hard, perhaps glad that I demanded their best and didn't pity them.

My best pupil was Todd. He had been a teacher before he went blind. With the training I provided, he became one of my teachers at Resource Incorporated. After I taught him computer programming, he could explain it better than people who have eyes. (Today Todd works at the Courage Kenny Rehabilitation Institute, which empowers people with disabilities to realize their full potential.)

Sadly, not everyone made it through the course. Each year I started with fifteen students, and during the nine months, five usually dropped out. But everyone who completed the course got a good, high-paying job. Because my students worked hard and learned so well, employers came to the school and started recruiting them after six months of training.

At that time, most new programmers earned $40,000 to $45,000 a year.

When I learned computers in prison, my instructors taught me Cobol, an old language that began around 1974, and changed only once in 1985. A number of business programs were written in Cobol, one of which was the system that ran the bus line. With the year 2000 coming up, many corporations needed Cobol masters. By then, most of the old Cobol programmers had died, retired, or moved on to other computer languages. That made my graduating students invaluable.

Since I worked with the county, I had access to their mainframe computers. So I gave my pupils experience working on them. They learned to run real-life programs and how to debug them.

I gave them assignments that were actual problems to solve, not just busywork. As a result, my pupils were a year ahead of four-year college graduates because those from the colleges didn't have real computer time or genuine work assignments.

Though I was still in the infant stages of my Christian growth, I knew I couldn't commit adultery again. I no longer wanted to have girlfriends, just a wife.

I was single again when I met Maury Latzer, who came from a wealthy family. I was a Christian and she was Jewish, but I really liked her. Her past had also been a difficult one, despite being the daughter of a wealthy man.

Maury's father, Sam, lived in Florida and invited both of us down several times. He liked me and I liked him. He was a well-educated man, and once said, "Even though you don't have a college degree, I consider you an informed man."

Sam and I had good conversations about world affairs and about business. We developed a deep friendship. In some ways, Sam was the father I didn't have. He was warm and generous and treated me like a son.

When I told some friends that I had fallen in love with Maury, one warned me that if I married her my faith would be compromised.

Another quoted 2 Corinthians 6:14: "Do not be yoked together with unbelievers. What do righteousness and wickedness have in common?"

I ignored their advice. Maury was deeply religious in her Jewish faith, but she knew about my commitment to Jesus and that didn't bother her. So it didn't bother me either.

I proposed, and she said, "Yes. But there's one condition. In the wedding ceremony, we can't have anyone mention the name Jesus. My family doesn't want you converting me."

She assured me that saying *God* would be fine. So I figured, what's the big deal if I don't say Jesus? I should have figured it out, but I was so in love with her I was blind to the issues and problems ahead. Instead, I sold Jesus down the river for that woman.

In the beginning, Maury and I had an excellent marriage. I was crazy about her and I know she loved me. Maury wasn't interested in Jesus, but she respected my faith and not once did she object to my going to church.

———

Years before we met, Maury had been a prostitute, as well as an alcoholic, but was now sober. She had been badly hurt when a client threw her out of his car. And several times she had been beaten and stabbed. Within a year after our wedding, she developed chronic back and shoulder pain because of those injuries.

The doctor gave her prescription painkillers and within months, Maury became addicted. One day, while I was at work, she took too many pills, went to the basement for something, passed out, and landed on her face. Her cheeks were badly bruised, and she broke her nose. She looked as if I had beaten her.

When I came home that afternoon, I found her downstairs, not fully conscious. I rushed her to the hospital where she stayed for a week.

When I told Sam what happened he flew to Minneapolis and visited Maury in the hospital.

Because she was afraid her father would cut her out of his will, Maury denied being addicted to prescription painkillers. When he asked her what happened, she said, "John beat me."

A few days later, one of Sam's lawyers filed an injunction and froze my bank account. That left me with no money.

The next day, another lawyer representing Sam came to my office. "You can get out of all this by signing here."

I looked at the form he handed me. "These are divorce papers," I said. "I don't understand."

"Maury's afraid of you, John. You've beaten her too many times. So we're not going to let you be around her again. We're moving her to Florida."

I was shocked. But I knew it would do no good to protest my innocence. I signed the papers. Maury took everything but my clothes.

Knowing Sam wouldn't talk to me, I didn't bother going to court.

Besides, I had been around enough addicts—and had been one myself. I didn't believe she could break her drug habit.

About a year after my wife divorced me and moved to Florida, Sam died. Maury, along with her brothers, was in Sam's will.

As part of her share of the inheritance, Maury received two large, mortgage-free houses, each worth about a million dollars. Not long afterward, she hooked up with a Cuban guy who was linked with the mob in Miami.

Once Maury's boyfriend learned she had money, he kept her locked in one of the houses. He fed her heroin to control her and forced her to sign a power of attorney. Then he and his friends cleaned out the bank account and sold both houses. Once she was penniless the boyfriend deserted her, leaving her homeless.

One day she called me and told me what had happened. "I'm really in trouble, John. My brothers won't even talk to me." Both brothers were independently wealthy, and angry she was an addict and had spent all of her inheritance.

I bought her a ticket to fly back to Minneapolis and I put her in rehab. She begged me to take her back into my life.

"I'll pay for everything," I said, "but I'm not getting involved with you again unless you graduate from treatment."

"I will quit, Johnny, I promise."

I wanted to believe her.

After she had been in treatment for twenty-one days, she did so well, they gave her a furlough. On her first day outside the rehab center she contacted her many wealthy friends, and one of them loaned Maury her apartment for the weekend. Maury went there on Friday afternoon and I was going to visit her the next morning.

About an hour before I left to go see her, Maury's friend called. "Maury overdosed. I found her dead a few minutes ago."

She had overdosed on Percocet, which at that time was expensive and hard to get. I wondered where Maury had gotten the drugs. She didn't have any money. She had several wealthy friends, but they all said they refused to give her any money until she was clean. I assumed she must have gotten the drugs because her family was well connected.

An autopsy, however, revealed that it wasn't the drugs that killed her. Maury had taken so many pills, she was like a walking zombie. And just as before, she tripped and fell flat on her face. This time the fall drove her nose bone into her brain.

I notified her brothers, and according to Jewish custom, she was buried within twenty-four hours. I arranged for a memorial service. None of her family members or friends came. Five or six people attended, but they were all my friends.

26

COPYCAT ROBBERIES

In late 1999, just before I finished teaching for the day, two police officers came to see me. "We have a warrant for your arrest," one of them said.

"What did I do wrong?"

"You committed five burglaries. Maybe more."

When he explained the details, I said, "I didn't do them." And I hadn't.

"We have eye witnesses," one of the detectives said. "And pictures."

I told him where I'd been at the time the burglaries happened.

Without checking my alibis, they took me to jail. I remained there for eighteen days without bail, awaiting trial.

Art harassed the arresting officer, the judge, everybody with any authority. But since I was still on parole from the sentence of eighty-five months, no one believed that I didn't do it. They all assumed I had come out of retirement and was stealing again. As a matter of fact, most of them thought I'd never stopped.

To make matters worse, the burglaries had all been done in a way similar to how I had once operated. What tagged me was that the man who committed the robberies first cased a building—just as I would have done.

After one of the crimes, the man got on an elevator with five lawyers. They all positively identified me as the person they had seen that day. "He had a suit on, a bald head, and a friendly smile," one witness said.

All the witnesses said, "The man was nice, friendly, and smiled. He didn't seem like someone who would commit robbery in our building."

A female security guard claimed that she had caught me coming out of a building, but I talked her into letting me walk away. "He was the nicest gentleman I'd ever met," she said. That fit my modus operandi.

Art came to the jail and asked the obvious question, "Did you do any of those crimes?"

"No," I said. "I didn't. I'm a Christian now."

Art believed me, without doubt or hesitation. That was encouraging. He was eager to help me. "Remember what I once told you," he said. "You won't have to defend yourself. I'm behind you."

My parole officer, however, didn't even come to visit me in jail because she believed I had messed up. That saddened me.

I prayed for God to vindicate me. During those eighteen days, I wondered if He was going to make me pay for my past sins, even though I was innocent this time. But if He had forgiven me, how could that be?

———

Art went to work on the judge and my PO, and when I came to court they were going to decide whether to violate me or not.

I told my lawyer, "I'm innocent. So in court, I want to answer any questions the police officer has without your advising me."

"That's stupid."

"But I didn't do anything wrong."

"It's still suicide. They're going to ask you questions just to see if they can trip you up on something."

"They can't trip me up because I didn't do it." I also firmly believed God would protect me.

My lawyer reluctantly agreed.

To my surprise, they didn't charge me in chronological order. When I testified in court, I pulled out the Day Planner I'd started using more than a year earlier. When I was asked about the burglary in which the lawyers allegedly saw me in the elevator, I looked up the date. My Day Planner showed that I was in Atlanta that day, at a conference on fatherhood. I remembered that I hadn't wanted to go because there would be three of us in a room, and I'd had enough of that in prison.

And because the other two men worked for Art and I didn't, I felt out of place. But Art insisted, so I went.

I gave the names of two ministers who had also been at the conference. Northwest Airlines verified my flights to and from Atlanta. My outgoing flight was within an hour of the time that crime was committed.

During the second burglary, I had been at an Urban Ventures board meeting because I was one of the star pupils who had come through the program. I spoke with former governor Al Quie and other board members about how important fathering was. Al Quie and the others verified that I had been there.

For the third charge, the prosecutor had a time-stamped picture. The photo was a little fuzzy, but the person in it did look somewhat like me. He was about my height and complexion.

But when I looked in my Day Planner there wasn't anything on that date because it was the same day I bought it.

A judge had ordered me to attend a seminar at my old treatment center, Eden House, for relapse prevention. The leader was a 3M executive. The meeting was on the importance of people in recovery using Day Planners to keep track of their time. So I bought one and brought it to the meeting.

The speaker was late, and when he finally arrived, I teased him. "Why didn't you use your Day Planner?"

We all laughed.

"What's your name?" he asked.

"Johnny Turnipseed."

"That's a unique name," he said.

"I'm writing a note here in my Day Planner that you were late." When I did just that, we laughed again.

"I see you're the only man here with a pen!" I was also the only attendee wearing a suit. I knew the speaker would remember me.

"That all-day seminar was the same day as this burglary," I said. "I couldn't have been in two places at the same time."

I showed the judge where I had scribbled on the front page of my Day Planner about the man from 3M being late.

The judge called for a recess so he could make some phone calls to verify the events written in my Day Planner.

About an hour later, the judge returned. After the court was called to order, he said, "His alibis check out."

They dropped all three charges.

That should have been the end. But about six months later, a detective called and told me another robbery with the same MO had taken place. He gave the date and asked, "Where were you?"

I checked my Day Planner. "I was in the fathering group. And my supervisor is right here."

I put my supervisor on the phone and he verified my presence.

Grumbling, the detective hung up.

A few weeks later, there was another copycat robbery, "You can't get out of this one, John," the detective said. A security guard had positively identified me as the man who walked out of the building with money and jewelry in my hands.

Once again, I checked my Day Planner. On the date in question, I'd gone to Omaha, Nebraska, because my nephew was in the hospital. My brother Jerome didn't have a car or any money, so I drove him there to see his son. When I got there, I realized I was out of money, so I stopped at an ATM and got cash.

When I told Art, he called the precinct. "John will turn himself in tomorrow."

The next day I went to the police station with my Day Planner, and the receipt from the ATM.

The security guard who had identified me stared at me, "I could have sworn it was you."

The detective, who knew about the former dropped charges, said, "You really are Mr. Day Planner and always have an alibi. But this is getting a little spooky." He peered at the pictures from the security cameras. "If this isn't you walking away from the scene, who is it?"

"I don't know," I said. And I didn't.

About a week later, the same detective called me again. "We ran the security camera's picture through our face-recognition program." He paused. "It appears you have a copycat. His name is Frank Jones."

I knew Frank. He used to date the younger sister of one of my former wives. He was my height, although about five years younger. Frank had always idolized me and followed my career. After I was busted he bought a suit and shaved his head, then started operating the same way I had.

The police arrested him.

God had protected me, and I couldn't stop praising and thanking him for it. I believe there are forces of evil as well as a force for God. I couldn't stop people from coming after me, but God could.

If there had been any wavering or doubt in me, after all those false charges were dropped, it was gone. That's when trust in God became cemented in my life.

———

Art believed me, and he put his reputation on the line for me. Ex-governor Al Quie did the same thing. At one time, he told me, "You have more integrity than anybody I've ever met." I still have two letters he wrote in support of me.

Al Quie also wrote to the current governor, asking for a full pardon for me. At the time of this writing, I'm still waiting on the answer.

———

Frank Jones went to prison and I never talked to him. After his release he disappeared. If he gets caught again, I suspect he'll say, "I didn't do that. It sounds like John Turnipseed." Not to intentionally put me in jail. But there's no honor among thieves, regardless of what they say.

27

HICCUPS AND GROWTH

I felt good about my standing with God. But everybody feels good when we get breaks and life is going well. I knew how to live as a Christian in principle, but not in practice. I didn't know if I could sustain my commitment to God over the long haul.

I felt like a soldier at boot camp. When the war hit, that's when I'd see whether I was a coward or a hero.

I hadn't faced a real war yet. Could I live day in and day out without going back to drugs or to the penitentiary?

I had a few hiccups along the way. I didn't do anything wrong enough to send me back to prison, but wrong enough to stiff my conscience.

For instance, one day I bought $300 worth of food stamps for $100. As soon as I did, I knew it was wrong. That day in my fathering group, I told the others what I had done.

"What's wrong with that?" one of them asked. "If you hadn't bought them, someone else would have."

I pointed out that I planned to use the food stamps for myself—to buy top-quality steaks and other fine foods. "It's a good deal, but it's a federal crime."

Everyone was quiet for a minute.

"Besides, the man who sold them to me obviously couldn't see Jesus in me. If he had, he wouldn't have approached me. What was it about my walk that said, 'I can approach this guy and ask him to be part of a felony'? He didn't approach other black men who passed him, but he walked right up to me. There was something about me that said I would buy those stamps. I need to figure that out."

That "hiccup" was an invaluable lesson for me. A little criminal was still running around inside me. And I didn't want to put up with that culprit.

———

In 1998, I received a phone call from Cary Cunningham, the chairman of the African American Men's Project for Hennepin County. I had done volunteer work for the county, and Mr. Cunningham said they were pulling together African American leaders in the community. Now that I was in the public eye, people knew who I was. I even had a nickname, John the Black Man.

Mr. Cunningham asked if I would be interested in becoming the director of the project. It was a high-level position, and it paid a lot of money.

Far more important than the money, this was a cause I believed in. Black men needed a makeover. We couldn't keep asking other people to do it for us; we had to do it ourselves. Even to this day I feel so strongly about that.

I accepted the job immediately and agreed to start the following Monday.

On Thursday, Art came to my office. He said he'd heard about my other job offer, and he asked me to work for him instead. He offered me half the pay and half the benefits of the other job. "They may want you," he said, "but we love you."

That sentence broke me. After all, Art had stood by me when no one else did. But I wanted to be sure of God's will. Money wasn't the issue. I really thought I might be of more use by working for the African American Men's Project. But I had to figure out which position God wanted me to take.

"I need a day to pray about this," I told Art. If I wasn't going to take the position, I felt I needed to tell them by Friday.

Art said he'd pray for me to make the right choice.

This wasn't the first time Art had asked me to work for him at the Center for Fathering. He'd made the same offer in 1995. At that time, I said that I was touched, but I had to decline. "I don't have the character yet to work for you. I don't want to mess up what you're trying to do. I'm a client and I need to work on me first."

But when Art asked this time, I was different. I had gone through trials and temptations with women, money, gambling, and drugs, and I was able to say no to all of them. I finally knew in myself that I would never go back to prison or to my old way of life.

In the beginning, I hadn't been sure if this Jesus thing would wear off after a while. I had never been in that water before. Now, I knew my commitment would last.

After a day of prayer, I accepted Art's offer. "I will never embarrass you," I promised him. And I meant it. I wasn't just trying to please him. It was a promise I made to him and to God. And I was a man of my word.

As I often tell others, when we surrender our lives to Jesus Christ, we don't know what's coming!

I knew my first challenge would be to convince people of my conversion.

Some people wouldn't believe I had changed, especially those that my family or I had hurt. And why would they? The Turnipseed violence had spread for four generations in Minnesota alone. From my dad, to me, to my son, and now my grandson, who is currently doing life without parole.

So I decided to become a licensed minister with the Church of God in Christ. I studied under Pastor Greg Baldwin and also went to school for a little more than a year and a half at a Bible College.

I didn't become a licensed minister so I could be a leader of a church. I did it so I could reach out to people in jail.

28

TEMPER TROUBLES

I know my shortcomings. One of them is that I still have a temper. I may not hit anyone over the head, but bullies infuriate me. If I see one picking on somebody, I'll stand up for that underdog, even if it puts me in danger.

One time, a major gangbanger leader I'll call Fred came to my fathering group. Fred was big and violent. His gang and I had once been enemies.

Whenever there was a pause in the conversation, Fred jumped in. Sammy, one of the men who reported to him, previously told me that Fred was still in his old life and wasn't truly part of the group.

Fred kept yelling at Sammy, who was a small man and didn't know how to handle it. So he apologized over and over. I wasn't going to let it go on, even though I knew Fred had four or five gangbangers outside the room.

"Leave Sammy alone, Fred," I demanded. "Why don't you pick on somebody your own size?" Nobody in the room was his size because he was a really big guy.

He stared at me. "Whatcha gonna do?"

"Man, I will hurt you." I walked over and stood close to him, inches from his face. "What are *you* going to do?"

Fred started moving around aggressively, like he was going to do something. If he punched me, I didn't know if I'd be able to retaliate. But because I wasn't afraid of him, I didn't move. I knew he wasn't going to kill me. The worst he could do was break a couple of bones. My stance was probably stupid, but I felt I had to protect Sammy.

Suddenly the big guy stopped, left the room, and went out to his gang. One of them later told me what happened.

"You gonna let that dude talk to me like that?" Fred asked.

"John's the chief," one of them said, which meant I was in charge, even though I didn't belong to his gang.

———

Another time, a big, violent man named Rudy came into my group. He called everyone names, though he didn't insult me the way he did the others.

When I'd had enough, I walked up to him and stared at him until he looked away.

"John Turnipseed," he yelled, "you're a punk and a fag!"

I laughed. "That's interesting. I haven't been called that combination before."

He got up and made a quick, aggressive move to see if I would flinch. I didn't. Instead, I took a step toward him and smiled. In a soft, quiet voice, I said, "Now you've really messed up. You've done made yourself look like a coward, man. You've got to do something."

Anger flashed in his eyes.

"You're thirty-five years old," I said, "and I'm over fifty. What are you going to do now, man?"

I was humiliating him because I had learned I could do more with my words than with my hands. I refused to back down and he wasn't able to strike at me.

"I don't know if you should go home tonight," I said. "Your friends are going to say, 'That old man stood you down. Why didn't you punch him?'"

I moved into his personal space and he backed up. I kept going forward and he kept backing up. I didn't stop until he was out of the building. I didn't cuss, just made him look small.

He never came back to the Center.

That encounter made me feel powerful. I wasn't aware of it at the time, but now I think that since I didn't have a father to stand up for me, I was filling the role of a protective father to the weaker men in my group.

Part of it probably also came out of my own sense of inadequacy and my fear of bullies when I was small. No one protected me in my growing-up years except for Tommy. I didn't have a true father figure until Dan Taylor, Father Capoochi, and especially Art Erickson came into my life.

Since I was bullied when I was a kid, the playground was the worst place in the world for me. Even girls beat me up. Talk about humiliation.

Once I started carrying a gun, bullies left me alone. And when I was older, I developed the ability to fight back. I became an above-average fighter and learned to take care of myself. And I had friends with me most of the time. They gave me the safety and security I didn't get from my father.

But bullies still made me angry. And I had a compelling need to disgrace them. I've since learned that switching roles is how some of us cope. We try to become for others what we needed others to be for us.

———

The board of the Center for Fathering sent me for further training to the National Center for Fathering in Kansas City. I represented Urban Ventures. My friend VJ Smith went to the class with me.

"African American men have lost the value of education. We don't treasure it anymore," the speaker said. "We no longer strive to be educated people and we're comfortable dropping out of school and settling for a GED."

That angered me. I had dropped out of school and got my GED. But I wasn't content with that. I was probably the only person in the room without a college education, and I felt put down.

"What you're saying is totally not true!" I yelled.

The speaker argued with me for a couple of minutes, and almost everybody started laughing.

He finally cut me off by saying, "But what you're saying is the most ridiculous thing I've ever heard."

I took that personally, and the way he said it upset me more than the words. "Well, that's my opinion, man."

"It's still stupid."

I got so mad I got up and left the room.

VJ came after me. "Chill out, John."

I fought to hold back my tears. I cry sometimes when I feel scared, and I didn't know what would happen if I started. I become like that poor kid in Selma, and later in Minneapolis, with no one to protect him.

Several minutes later, the speaker came out of the room. "Can I talk to you?" he asked quietly.

"No."

"Come on," VJ said, "at least speak with him. He's teaching the class after all."

I nodded, and we went into his office. "If I have offended you in any way, my brother, I'm sorry," he said. "I really am. I apologize for anything I did in that room that hurt you. I wish I could take it back, but I can't. Would you please forgive me?"

He was sincere. I wondered if he was only apologizing because he knew I could beat him up and he was afraid. "Don't ever talk to me like that again."

"I won't. I'm truly sorry, brother."

"All right then." I refused to shake his hand because I was still angry. I got up to leave his office. *He's lucky, I could have hurt him bad.*

Just then, I noticed a beautiful plaque with gold writing on it hanging on his wall. He was a martial arts master. He could have wiped the floor with me. But he didn't.

He backed down when he didn't need to. He was strong enough to apologize and let me save face. He defused the fight when he could have won easily.

Most men, when they have the upper hand, don't back down. And this guy clearly had the upper hand. He was younger and stronger, and with all the martial arts behind him, he could have disabled me quickly. Instead, he was gentle, without being condescending.

That speaker taught me a powerful lesson through that gesture. A man who is sure of himself takes care of other men.

Since that time, I've tried to deal with situations in the same way he did. It takes a lot of courage to not be macho when you have the upper hand.

29

MAD DADS

I'm an imperfect disciple of Jesus Christ, and my temper is probably my worst failing. It even got me in trouble during press conferences and interviews I conducted as a representative of Urban Ventures.

At one press conference, I felt that the neighborhood "alligators"—the people who received the government funds—were taking advantage of the poor people in our community. A tornado had come through North Minneapolis and destroyed houses. A lot of money came in for federal grants, but none of the poor people received any. Some were still living with tarps over their houses, while those in better neighborhoods received up to $50,000 each. The government spent around $2 million in that community, but none of the poor people I knew benefited.

I addressed that in the press conference—with a lot of anger in my voice. I should have toned it down, but I was incensed over the way the poor had been pushed aside.

At the end of the conference, the money man, an African American, was also angry as he walked over to where I was seated. He leaned forward and whispered, "We know how to deal with niggers like you."

I hadn't done anything to this man, but my reputation had preceded me. He knew my family. His derogatory comment referred to people who would do violent things to get what they want.

I felt uncomfortable having a man standing over me, jabbing his finger in my chest and making threats. I was so angry, but all I did was stand and stare at him. Immediately, he backed up. And three of his men jumped in front of me, to protect him in case I tried to hit him.

For some reason, I started crying. Even though cameras were all around, I couldn't stop.

Please, God, get me out of here.

I walked out of the room, without saying a word.

To my surprise, people remembered—not my being a crybaby who walked away—but commended me for standing up for the poor people in our neighborhood. I received many pats on the back for not acting the fool.

One of the great joys in my redeemed life is to work with great friends like VJ Smith. Here's a brief look at his history.

He is one of those individuals who, like me, should be dead or in prison for the rest of his life.

VJ's mother rejected him when he was nine years old. "I don't want you," she said. "And I can't feed you." She drove him to the juvenile center and told him to get out of her car. "Now go inside. They'll take care of you."

In effect, he became an orphan that day.

After going through the court system, VJ got into running drugs and guns for a major gang in Kansas City. To avoid a long prison sentence, he ran away, and ended up in Minnesota. He worked as a radio DJ, and later, as a baggage handler in what was then Northwest Airlines.

VJ met a woman named Ruthie and she invited him to church. God convicted VJ of his sinful ways, and he surrendered his life to Jesus Christ.

Art met VJ at a community meeting and invited him to the group I was teaching at the Center for Fathering. That's where I met him.

VJ told me his initials meant Victory for Jesus. He had an outgoing personality, and he wanted to be a group facilitator, so I let him speak at group meetings. He gained respect from everyone. He soon became my best friend.

When VJ learned about MAD DADS,* he talked to me about forming a chapter in Minneapolis. Without hesitating, I agreed.

Members of MAD DADS pray for people on the streets. They care about the young people and don't want them to go through the trauma we experienced.

They also do volunteer security for the Mall of America, the biggest shopping center in the United States. They wear green shirts so they're easily identified. A lot of young black kids go there, and they could easily get into trouble. But our people know how to handle them. "Just chill out," they might say. But it's more than just their words, members of MAD DADS are respected, even by the gangs, and no one messes with them.

Currently, we're putting on a benefit for a poor family whose house was burned down. Our people don't have a lot of financial resources, but they do what they can. When we put out a call, we might raise up to $500. That may not sound like much, but it can go a long way in helping them reestablish themselves—money they wouldn't have if Urban Ventures hadn't come along. Whereas, a middle-class white family would probably raise $10,000.

My friend VJ is now the national president of MAD DADS. He's done an amazing job, and I'm very proud of him.

———————

VJ and I have done other things together, including putting together a radio show called *Street Soldier,* for urban people to talk about what's going on in their neighborhoods. We soon had a big following, and sponsors wanted to get behind us.

After a few months, the station manager told me, "This show is so good we can take it nationally."

———————

* **MAD DADS** was founded in 1989 by African American men who were fed up with gang violence and the flow of illegal drugs into their community. Members of **MAD DADS** promote and demonstrate positive images of fathers engaging in community development and protecting youth and families.

VJ and I were excited . . . until he said, "But we'll need to use more seasoned people."

He took the show away from us.

I felt like I had been stabbed in the heart. VJ and I had thought up the idea, and we knew the people we wanted to reach. We were doing something positive for the community. And as soon as the program became successful, they took it away from us. Once we'd built up an audience, they didn't need us anymore.

There was nothing we could do about it. So we let it go without a fight.

The show lasted about a month before our sponsors pulled out. They had backed it because they liked VJ and me. Those so-called seasoned professionals couldn't sustain the program, let alone elevate it to a national level.

After that, VJ and I started *Street Talk* on cable television as a reality show. We film conversations with people on the streets. We also go to crack houses, and many men and women have gone into treatment through our efforts. One year, we documented at least fifty people in Minneapolis who became sober because of what we were doing.

On the streets, folks now call me Rev. And with my gang history I'm able to go into all of the gang territories. I'm "one of God's boys," they say. "And God's boys get a pass."

Getting a pass applies to any religious group, even the young Mormons in white dress shirts who canvass the black neighborhoods on their $200 bicycles. No one takes their wallets or steals their bikes. "We don't want to bring the wrath of God on ourselves," the gangs have often said.

30

THE NEW JOHN TURNIPSEED

God has given me favor and influence among people who used to honor me as a gang leader. For example, in 2008, I attended a funeral for a friend. Reverend Bill, a secretive drug addict, was asked to conduct the service.

The day of the funeral, one of my cousins called. "I'm holding Reverend Bill. He owes us $2,500. But he says he's supposed to do a funeral this afternoon. Is that true?"

"Yes, it is. I'm going to it."

"Well, he ain't gonna make it, Johnny, not unless you're willing to vouch for him and pay us."

"I'm not going to pay his debt." He needed to face his own responsibilities.

"We ain't lettin' him go until his wife gets off work with her paycheck, cashes it, and hands us our money."

At the funeral, I told the family members of my deceased friend, "I'm sorry, but Reverend Bill won't be here today."

"Why not?" one asked.

"I don't want to get into the details. Let's just say he's in a bad situation."

"What are we going to do?"

"If it's all right with you, I can conduct the funeral."

"Are you a minister?"

"Yes, I am."

"Then that's okay."

I stood in front of the crowd, five or six of whom were people

I knew from my old life who didn't know I'd changed. As I stood to speak, one of them yelled, "Man, who's this?" He told everyone about something I had done to him. Someone else cussed at me. A third person told people about the women I had slept with and the drugs I'd sold.

I let them talk and made no effort to deny anything. But as they spoke, I prayed silently and asked for God's favor.

As the noise quieted, I said, "For God so loved the world that he gave his only begotten Son, that whosever believeth in him—*even Johnny Turnipseed*—should not perish but have everlasting life."*

My detractors stared at me in unbelief.

"My God is big enough to do anything with anybody, and He changed my life. Now He's chosen me to deliver this sermon. I want you to honor my God because I'm one of His."

No one said a thing.

I wasn't prepared to give a sermon. But I knew I could rely on God to pull me out of this impossible situation. So I preached a short, simple message.

When I finished, I received a standing ovation.

After that, a number of individuals started calling me Reverend, Minister, or Pastor Turnipseed. The title didn't mean much, but it convinced me that even the die-hard scoffers recognized that I had changed.

———

My brother Jerome was known as the most sensible and nicest of the Turnipseed brothers. He died of alcoholism at age forty-eight. At his funeral in 2008, my mother said, "All of my boys are ruthless, except my gentle one and he's gone."

The day Jerome died, I was getting ready to preach a sermon at the Center for Fathering and forgot to turn off my cell. Just before I went to speak, the phone rang. Normally I would have turned it off, but for some reason, I answered.

"Jerome is in the hospital," one of my brothers said. "And it's bad. Real bad."

---

* John 3:16 KJV.

I told him I'd get there as quickly as I could, but I had to preach a sermon first. When I reached the hospital, I learned that Jerome had died before my brother called.

Probably eighty people were gathered around. But the hospital staff refused to let me see Jerome's body. I figured security didn't know how to deal with so many large, agitated black men.

I asked the guard to let me talk to the man in charge. He hesitated. But because I spoke good English and was wearing a suit, he called the chief of security and handed me the phone.

When I introduced myself, the chief of security recognized my name because of the work I'd done with Urban Ventures. After a brief conversation, I handed the phone back to the guard. I overheard the chief say, "John Turnipseed will handle this. Tell the security staff to leave." And they did.

My family had trouble facing the reality of Jerome's death. Some yelled profanities, while others slammed their fists into the walls. Many cried openly and loudly.

For almost a month, I prayed for my family members and did what I could to calm them down, holding my own emotions inside. But one day, I broke down and the tears flowed. I thought of the way David in the Bible wept for his lost son Absalom. Even though Jerome was my brother, I had been his father figure. I felt as if I had lost my own child.

I also wept for myself. My father had left a wound that would never be repaired. Jerome's death tore open that wound. It also made me realize that I could never reclaim my lost childhood.

My dad never once hugged me. My mother never hugged me either, but I never doubted her love. I grieved over not having my father's affection as a child, knowing that hole would always remain.

For two days I lay in bed and sobbed. I couldn't eat. I slept only when I was too exhausted to cry. I felt totally powerless and worthless, unable to take care of myself. I prayed, but I was in too much pain to connect with God.

After two days of wanting to die, I slowly emerged from my grief. God was with me. And—for now at least—my pain was receding.

As I came out of my protracted grief, I realized more powerfully than ever why I wanted to help younger men. I couldn't replace their fathers, but I could become the one male figure in their lives who cared and expressed that compassion.

———

In my old life I handled problems violently, but now I handle them differently. For example, a relative named Bam, called me in tears, and said, "My boyfriend, Jamal, beat me, and he molested my daughter." She also said that he used drugs in front of her children.

In my family, we don't call the police for that. But in the old days, we would have beaten him real bad, maybe even killed him. Now that I'd changed, I wanted to model a godly approach.

I called three of my brothers, and they went with me to Bam's house. For years we had traveled together for family matters, but this time we took no guns.

We went over in the middle of the night, while everyone was asleep. We snuck into the house and found Jamal's bodyguard, a tough man who carried a big gun, snoring in a drunken stupor.

After taking his gun, we went upstairs. I pulled Jamal out of bed.

He grinned and said, "You're a preacher. You ain't gonna do nothin' to me."

I wanted to break his neck. If I had given them permission, my brothers would have gladly shot Jamal with his bodyguard's gun. Not many crimes are as low as molesting a child and it would have been easy to go back to my old ways.

"Little Johnny is the only rider in our family," Jamal said with a smirk. (A rider is one who will shoot you.) "And he's in jail. So ain't nothin' you can do!"

In a calm voice, I said, "Wake up your drunken friend downstairs, and both of you get out of here. And don't come back." I pushed him out the bedroom door.

Jamal never went back to Bam's house.

When Bam's friends heard that she'd called me in to deal with Jamal, they were shocked to hear that I hadn't killed him, or at least hurt him.

"John's different now," she explained.

Shortly after that, Jamal was arrested for kidnapping a twelve-year-old girl and taking her across the state line. I'm glad the pervert is locked up. But I'm also glad I didn't take vengeance into my own hands.

31

SERVICES AND SUCCESSES

I started working for Urban Ventures as director of the Center for Fathering three years after I turned to Jesus Christ in 1995. At first, I was in charge of day-to-day operations and teaching fathers how to be better parents. I began by developing close relationships with five men, mentoring them one-on-one. I required at least three face-to-face meetings each month, but I made myself available whenever they wanted to see me.

At the height of my mentoring, I was responsible for about twenty young men. These friends strengthened me to stay focused on the Lord even while I concentrated on guiding them.

Many of those I mentored came from prison. They'd heard about me, and what I did, and the word was out that I could be trusted. Those men, like me, had been cheated many times, so trust didn't come easily.

In addition to counseling, I helped them get jobs, went to court with them, and supported them, even when they were guilty. Often, I was their only positive character reference. I found that the best time to help them was when they had to face the reality of their situations.

When I was able to get them probation, the court assigned them to the Center for Fathering. That gave me leverage. I faced few problems with those men because they were grateful that somebody would stand up for them.

One time I helped one of my mother's friends, Tawarna Richardson, who dated one of my brothers. Mom asked me to advocate for her, so I stepped in.

Tawarna was in prison for killing a man who had assaulted her.

In the height of her anger, someone gave her a gun, and she used it to shoot her abuser. When he ran, she chased him and shot him again. The judge offered her ten years, but her lawyer told her, "We can beat this." She listened to him—and got a life sentence.

Tawarna was so angry the prison guards kept writing her up. When she appeared before the parole board, they turned her down. As a result, she spent six more years in prison.

That's when my mother asked me to intervene. I called the Commissioner of Corrections and asked if I could see Tawarna. He agreed. After our meeting, I went to the parole board hearing with Tawarna and presented her case. Against the recommendations of the prison staff, the commissioner released her to me, which is unusual.

Tawarna became a Christian and reunited with her family. She has been out of prison for almost a decade. In all those years, she never had a relapse. Tawarna is one of my joy stories. She worked faithfully for me for three years.

I'm willing to help any man or woman who is open. I don't care if they come from gangs or have just gotten out of prison. Because of my past, they know they can trust me to help them.

Another good example is my nephew Rappy Rodney. In 2007, he stole a car with a sleeping baby in the backseat. The police caught him and charged him with kidnapping. Conviction for child kidnapping is an automatic prison sentence, and he should have received fifteen years.

I went to the district attorney and said, "As a personal favor, please be lenient with him."

Because the DA knew me and was aware of my helping African Americans, he granted him probation.

I expressed my deep gratitude with my biggest smile.

I wanted the Center for Fathering to reach black men like me. So I used a concept I found in the Bible. When God wanted to deliver the Jews out of Egypt, He sent a Jew to do it. So I hired five African Americans who came out of the same background I did.

I needed to build the reputation of the Center for Fathering as a safe place for men. The government started to take notice of us after we reached a number of men, especially when we helped turn ex-cons into honest members of society.

But I didn't believe that only African Americans could work with blacks. After all, I'd had three wonderful mentors—Art Erickson, Dan Taylor, and Father Capoochi—who helped me at different periods of my life. All of them are college educated. None of them are black or has ever been locked up. Yet they were the biggest influences in my life.

After two or three years of working at the Center, I hired a white man, Don Constable, a seventy-year-old rocket scientist from Boise, Idaho. He had never worked around black people in his life, but he had no problem being the first Caucasian at the Center.

Once we were established, I started hiring women. Although 90 percent of our targeted population is African American males, I've intentionally made my staff diverse. We now have people of every ethnic background including five non-black women, one of whom is Spanish. My secretary, Julie Grengs, is white, and so is my boss. At one time we had a white director who specialized in writing grant proposals.

As we grew, I widened our scope to include anyone with certain skill sets who wanted to help.

I've been outspoken on this. And as a black man, I can also criticize other African Americans. At various times I met other blacks whom I wanted to be around and learn from, but they didn't have any time or interest in me.

A few years ago, I was in a gathering of nearly forty African American men engaged in social work. I'd known many of them for years and I'd been in their programs. I thanked them, then said, "Not one of you guys ever took me aside and said, 'I see something good in you, Johnny.'"

Several were offended and others were defensive, but I didn't retreat. "It means we have failed our own people. We have mentoring organizations and yet we can't find black mentors."

My three white mentors worked extra hard to break down prejudicial barriers to get to me. But it would have been nice to have someone of color who was concerned for my welfare.

At the Center for Fathering, we open our arms to everyone. We now have men from all walks of life who come to our meetings. And no one has ever said to me, "I'm uncomfortable here."

The community holds us in high esteem. In twenty years, no one has ever been assaulted, and gangs don't graffiti our property.

People respect us, in large part because they admire Art, who has worked in this neighborhood for nearly fifty years. He probably has more black friends than Caucasian ones. When he passes away, the black people who line up at the door will easily outnumber the others. Art earned their admiration and love by staying.

Art calls this area his "peanut." That's a reference to the work of George Washington Carver, who focused on the lowly peanut and never gave up. He was an African American who was almost solely responsible for the rise in US peanut production after the boll weevil devastated the South's cotton crops.

Art says he took this area as his peanut, and there's so much to do here that he'll never get it all done. We wouldn't move even if we were offered millions of dollars.

Nor do we have any plans to replicate this organization. The talent base needed to continually respond to needs is hard to put together in one place. Although we're not a perfect organization, we're making inroads and doing well. Managing three or four Centers for Fathering would deplete our energies and efforts.

We have established a model in which we're open to help others get a group started. And we encourage others to copy what we're doing. We'd love to see them succeed.

Any such work has to build on the foundation of trust, and people in Minneapolis have learned to trust us. We'll visit a son or a brother in jail who wants help from a minister. If a riot breaks out, and someone gets shot and calls the police, we get there as quickly as we can to intervene and calm the crowds. We're well-known as the place where people of all colors can get help.

Our clients come from all over the Twin Cities. Some ride a bus ten miles to get to us. Our support groups are growing, and it's not unusual for 100 people to show up at a single event.

No one is afraid to come to us. We guarantee safety, even to those who come from gangs that are enemies with the Bloods. My family knows this is where I work and, therefore, will not harm anybody who enters our offices.

For a center like ours to succeed, we have to be willing to confront bad behavior. And we can make a powerful difference in whether someone kills or not.

Sometimes people say to me, "I want to be more like Jesus."

"No, you don't," I tell them. "Jesus hung out with sinners and was the toughest man who ever lived. That dude was a warrior."

They don't usually get what I mean, so I add, "Suppose you met someone and you positively knew he would betray you and cause your death if you accepted him. Would you still love that individual?"

"No way," is the usual answer.

"Well, that's what Jesus did. He opened His heart to Judas, taught him, empowered him to heal the sick, and sent him out alongside the other disciples. All the time, Jesus knew Judas would betray Him, but He loved the man so much, He withheld nothing." Then I add, "I couldn't do that either. But maybe one day, I can love with that capacity."

32

SAFE PASSAGE

Two of the lieutenants from Chicago's Gang Disciples were shot when they visited Minneapolis. The GDs declared a gang war that involved our part of the city. I didn't want anyone else to die.

I told the board of directors for Urban Ventures, "I'd like to offer the GDs safe passage to the Center for Fathering so we can talk to leaders from both gangs."

After a little discussion, the board agreed.

I invited the GD leaders from Chicago to come for a meeting to see if we could stop the gang war. They accepted. I then called the Bloods, since Urban Ventures is part of their territory. The Bloods agreed to give the GDs safe passage.

With careful moderating, the contingent from Chicago met and agreed not to retaliate for the deaths of their two lieutenants, and left the city without incident.

That's the type of thing I can do.

I'm a Christian and no longer part of the underworld, but by the grace of God, I still have influence. Most of the young Bloods call me Uncle Johnny, to show their respect for my position. At the present time I'm the second-oldest living male Turnipseed. Both of us have very high rank.

I don't agree with what the gang does, and I hate their violence. But they know I will help them in anything that's lawful. They won't consult me about doing anything illegal, but there are times when they really want my influence.

For example, let's say my nephew Paulie was wanted for murder, and wanted to turn himself in. Paulie couldn't take a bus to the police station because he might get shot when he passed through other gang territories. (Most of my family members can't take the city bus.) But once Paulie (or anyone) passes Lake Street, which is near our offices and is open and safe, he could come to me. And if he did, I could arrange safe passage. They regard me as "God's boy," and anybody with me is covered. To this day, that area is still safe.

My youngest brother, Markalow, is safe anywhere as long as he's traveling with me. I have to give him a ride to and from my groups because it's not safe for him to ride the bus.

In 2013, a rival gang shot three Bloods—because they were outside the area—killing one and paralyzing the other two.

Every day—without exception—I must live according to God's laws. If I deviated by doing anything illegal, the word would spread, and within days I'd lose all respect.

Despite my influence, not everyone heeds my advice. For example, Kevin, Little Johnny's best friend, was accepted as part of the Bloods even though he wasn't a family member. One day Kevin spotted Lamar in our territory. For ten years, a family member of ours had wanted Lamar killed. So Kevin raced down the street in his car, and as he got close, he sprayed Lamar with bullets and killed him. A stray bullet hit a little cousin who was innocently standing on the street. It entered his head and he died.

Here's where the trouble came into play. The Bloods wanted Lamar dead, but Kevin killed a family member. A basic rule of all gangs is that if you kill a group member, you die. Even if it was an accident.

Gang members told Little Johnny he had to kill his best friend.

"I ain't gonna do that. He didn't mean to kill the boy."

"Don't matter. It's your job to kill Kevin."

"I won't do it!"

"Then you're an outcast."

Little Johnny was kicked out of the Bloods and had to leave the territory. And Kevin was on the Bloods' hit list. By gang rules, they were right, and only by holding to such rules do gangs survive and stay strong.

One day, Kevin braked his car for a stop sign. Two Bloods, brothers William and Ames, walked over and emptied their guns. They didn't kill Kevin, but they accidentally killed Kevin's cousin, who was a passenger in the car.

Kevin was willing to testify against William and Ames. After a big manhunt, which was widely publicized in the news media, the authorities caught the brothers. They hired a gang lawyer.

Some lawyers are willing to defend gang members, and they sometimes get paid in girls and drugs. It's a lucrative business since that attracts more gang business. And gangs have money.

The DA offered William and Ames ten years in prison.

"Take it," I told them. "It's a good deal, and you can get out in seven years."

However, they refused the offer on the advice of their lawyer. They are now both serving life sentences. Despite the term, *life* means they must do thirty years before they're eligible for parole. Even if the brothers get parole, they will have to serve an additional fifteen years for being members of a gang when they committed the crime.

———

Pookie, a once-famous pimp was hard and ruthless, and had idolized me when he was a kid. In his heyday, he drove expensive cars, surrounded himself with glamorous women in mink coats, and regularly went to places like Las Vegas to gamble.

When one of his girls tried to run away, he burned the insides of her legs and her crotch with a hot iron. That was his trademark punishment, and a warning to other girls not to leave. "She'll be so nasty," he once boasted to me, "she'll never open her legs for another man."

Pookie was prosecuted for burning two girls, and served two sentences of ten years to life in federal prison. However, at age fifty-four, he received parole.

Shortly after his release, several family members had a picnic, and they invited Pookie. I didn't attend, but I heard that a handful of boys sat next to Pookie. "Tell us pimp stories," they begged.

"I'm not into that any more," he said.

"We came just to meet you," one boy said.

"C'mon, you're a legend," a second said.

"I want to learn to pimp girls," a third kid added. "And everyone says you're the best."

To Pookie's credit, he refused to help them. "I've reformed, and I'm trying to do honest work."

Unfortunately, Pookie had trouble finding a job. Nobody wants to hire an ex-pimp that badly hurt two of his prostitutes.

Right now, he holds a low-paying construction job, for which he doesn't have the build. But he has never held a real job before, and this was all he could get.

He is also going to school and we're trying to help him. I hope he doesn't revert to his old ways.

My friend VJ of MAD DADS, who is now the chief of police, once asked me to speak at a prison near Fairbolt, Minnesota. About 100 inmates attended. After the program finished, the facilitator told me, "John, one of the inmates says he needs to talk to you."

"Sure," I said. "Who is he?"

"His name is James Earl."

James Earl had received a prison sentence of fifteen years for shooting off my son's leg. I hadn't seen him in a long time.

When the man came forward, I stared. If the facilitator hadn't told me who he was, I'm not sure I would have recognized him. He was older than when I last saw him, but he'd also gotten bigger and more muscular.

Without thinking about it, my true character came out. I walked over to James and hugged him—something I do best. Immediately, I heard the clicks and saw the flashes of the cameras.

I wondered if the facilitator had orchestrated this meeting, since he had grown up with me, and he knew how much I loved Little Johnny. I'm sure he assumed I'd be angry and create a scene, but he didn't get what he expected. God had His protecting hand on me.

"I didn't do that to your son," James said when we finished hugging.

I knew it was a lie because Little Johnny had seen him standing over him, laughing before he shot him again. But I said, "It's in the past and no longer matters."

I hugged James a second time, and for a moment, the room went quiet.

The next time I went to visit Little Johnny, he showed me a picture somebody sent him of me hugging the man who shot him. I felt like somebody had jolted me with a cattle prod. I told Little Johnny what happened.

"Even though I figured I'd been set up," I said, "I needed to hug James. That's the only way I knew how to prove that I've forgiven him for what he did to you."

33

SOMETIMES WE FAIL

Individuals often walk into my office who have done favors for me or my family in the past.

One time, the man who put the hit out on Little Johnny came in, not knowing I worked there. When he saw me, the fear on his face left no doubt that he realized that I knew what he had done. It looked like he was going to run. So I grabbed him and hugged him.

Hugs are powerful and most of us can feel how you mean them. If I hug a woman with a sexual intent, she'll know it. If I hug her like a father, she'll know it. I also believe that when I embrace a man to show I've forgiven him, he'll know how I feel.

This man's body stiffened and he started to do that man thing, patting my shoulder, but I held him gently and said, "How you doing?"

"Oh, okay, okay." He wasn't at ease, but he was no longer on high alert.

I invited him into my office, and we talked. He said he needed a job. I offered to assist him with that.

"Sure. Okay," he said. But he never came back to take the job I found for him.

Although disappointed, I had to remind myself that I had done my best for him. I was not responsible for his actions.

Willie Lloyd was another visitor from the past who came to my office at the Center for Fathering in 2013. He's the man who, in 1970, shot Sheron twice when she was pregnant with my daughter Lisa. When he got out of prison he came to the Center for help.

Willie was another person who didn't know I worked there until he saw me. The scared look on his face, told me he wanted to run, but I reached out my hand. Reluctantly he shook it. While shaking hands, I pulled him close and hugged him. "Man, you okay?"

"Yeah." But he didn't look okay.

"What do you need? What can I do for you?"

After a brief and uncomfortable conversation, I bought him a bus card. I hoped that would show him that I had moved on and didn't hold a grudge.

He mentioned the shooting and started to apologize. I stopped him. "It's all right. I forgave you a long time ago."

When I tell people about my many success stories, sometimes they ask, "Do you have any failures?"

"More than I'd like to admit," I say. "Even one failure is tragic, but there are many."

For instance, a drug dealer named Lee came to my office about ten years ago, only because coming to the Center was his get-out-of-jail-free card. In our first meeting, he said, "I hate you, man, and I hate everything you stand for."

"Stand in line, Lee. I don't like me much either."

Because I made a joke out of it, he settled down a little.

Lee came to the Center faithfully, as required in order to get out of jail. The entire time he'd sit, arms folded across his chest, and glare at me, as if to say, "I dare you to say anything I like."

To my surprise, after his mandatory attendance was over, Lee kept coming to the meetings. One day he pulled me aside. "You know, you're all right."

With those simple words, Lee and I started a relationship. I tried to be to him what Art was to me.

Lee had three children, all in the custody of his ex-wife. She was one of those rare women with no maternal instincts. The kids were constantly exposed to drug dealers, pimps, and pedophiles. When Lee opened up to me, he said, "I just want to go over there, kill everybody in the house, and pull my kids out of there."

Calmly I said, "If you will just trust us, we'll fight for your children. If that doesn't work, then you can try your way."

Afterward, I thought those were bold words and maybe the wrong thing to say. But Lee was already wanted for murder in another state. Because the authorities in that state didn't want anything to do with him, they made no attempt to extradite him.

As Lee and I built a good relationship over the next year and a half, I was able to help him gain custody of all three children. Faithfully, he went to church with me and brought his children. I helped him get a job at our Center. I was so proud of Lee, in my mind he became the poster child for father of the year.

But Lee still had a temper. One time he became angry and insulted a client. When he refused to apologize, I had to fire him. He understood, and we're still friends. Slowly we lost contact—or, more accurately, he dropped out of my life.

Nearly two years ago, Lee called me, but something didn't sound right. As I listened, I realized he was slurring.

"I want you to come and see me. Right now," I said.

When he got to my office, he said, "I got in a car accident." When I didn't respond, he said, "I went to a doctor and he gave me a prescription for Percocet."

Everyone in our community knew how the system worked. Insurance companies will readily pay $10,000 for a car accident. But if doctors get involved, the medical costs can quickly grow to $30,000. Most of the time, the insurance company would rather pay the $10,000 and leave the doctors out of it.

Whenever there was a car accident in our neighborhood, the parties involved rushed to a doctor, whether injured or not. "My neck hurts. So does my back. Everything hurts. I'm sure I have whiplash." No one can prove they're not in pain.

That process was called the Ghetto Fabulous. I knew that's what Lee had done. Although I suspect he wasn't really hurt, the insurance company paid him the money.

Lee had been a heroin addict, but he'd been sober for thirteen years. Unfortunately, only one Percocet brought his habit back, and soon he was taking them like gumdrops. When the prescription ran out, he used his insurance money to buy large quantities of drugs, like heroin, and sold a lot of them so he could keep most of the money.

When Lee realized that his addiction to heroin was affecting his three children, he came to the Center. It broke my heart to see him like that. Art and I prayed fervently for him and rallied behind him.

Lee agreed to go into detox, but he left after a few days. I took him to different treatment centers, but he never stayed. I finally lost track of him.

A few months later, Lee called at one o'clock in the morning, "I'm at the hospital. My baby is in a coma."

"I'll be right there." I was still half-asleep when I got to the hospital. "What happened?"

"He got into my dope," Lee said, "and he overdosed." Lee sat there, looking lost.

His ten-year-old son obviously loved his father, and said he had called 911. A neighbor was watching the daughter while they were at the hospital.

"Did you tell the doctors about the drugs?"

Lee shook his head. "They think he had some kind of asthma attack."

"You've got to tell them," I said, "or your boy may die."

"But they'll get me for possession."

"Which is more important? The police not arresting you or saving the life of your son?"

The baby was in a coma for two hours before Lee confessed. "Thank you," the doctor said. "That's what I needed to know."

The child recovered. The police didn't arrest Lee, but they took all three children into protective custody.

That was a terrible time for Lee. His guilt overwhelmed him, which pushed him deeper into his addiction. I talked and prayed with him but got nowhere. I stayed his friend, but he no longer came around, and I understood. I assumed he was just one of those people who didn't have the capacity to live free of drugs.

But Lee's story isn't over. When Lee contacted me again, I found out that he eventually got sober and regained custody of his children. The four of them were living in a homeless shelter. They had food and a place to sleep, but rats and cockroaches took over in the dark, and it's probably the worst-run shelter I've ever seen.

Art and I helped Lee find a job and got him into a three-bedroom, two-bathroom condo for fifty dollars a month.

But he soon fell back into his old ways and lost his job and the condo. He returned to the shelter. Although they let the kids stay, they kicked him out.

Lee entrusted me with what was left of his insurance money. I dole it out as he needs it and he can live almost a week on twenty bucks.

All the children are in school. The boy who overdosed hears voices at night telling him to kill himself. He's just a lost kid. The older son is struggling in school. The girl seems to be the only normal one among them.

Today, Lee is a shell of the proud man he used to be. I still feel sad when I think of him. He was my shining star, my trophy of success. But then he lost everything.

Lee says, "I believe God is still the Lord of my life."

And I believe he's sincere—weak and struggling—but sincere in his desire to be whole. In his case, the last chapter hasn't been written on his story. I'm still praying for a happy ending.

34

DEEP DISAPPOINTMENTS

I wish I could say Lee's story was the rare exception, but it's not. I've worked with several men who start well, but can't seem to finish the race. The only way they finally make it is for someone to continuously work with them. This has to be someone who cares deeply and will do anything for them. Maybe that's why I've stayed around the Center.

I also stay for myself because, as the apostle Paul warns, "So, if you think you are standing firm, be careful that you don't fall!"*

I have constant support myself. I know I'm strong enough that I could do well on my own, but I'm a lot stronger with my network of friends to help me.

Despite the support, it hasn't been easy for me. I often wonder why God would use me. What did I ever do to deserve such kindness? Those questions can't be answered except to call it God's grace.

For example, in 2006, Art scheduled me to speak to a large meeting at the Center for Fathering. A number of dignitaries would be present. I spent a lot of time preparing what I hoped would be a powerful message.

The day before the event, a voice in my head whispered, "You're not anything. You'll make a fool out of yourself. Those people will laugh at you."

Maybe it the devil speaking, but whatever it was, I lost any sense

---

* 1 Corinthians 10:12.

of self-worth. I felt like nothing. "I can't do it," I cried out. "What do I have to say?"

I went to bed with a heavy heart, knowing I was not worthy and that I couldn't speak at that meeting. But I was afraid to tell anyone how I felt.

About three o'clock in the morning, I woke up and started crying. I crept out of the bedroom so my wife wouldn't hear me.

That accusing voice yelled, "Go ahead and cry, you little baby! Finally you realize that you're nothing."

Not knowing how to silence that tormenting voice, I turned on the TV and immediately the smiling face of Joel Osteen stared at me.

My wife loved watching him, but I could never sit through a whole program. I detested that man. "Nobody can be that happy," I muttered. "Nobody!"

As I started to change the channel, the camera focused on Osteen's face, and as close as I can remember, he said: "They've told you you're too short, too quiet, not big enough, not bold enough, you've got a speech impediment. And they've told you that you're not worthy, that you can't do it, that you shouldn't be who you think you are, that you're nothing. But God has a bigger plan for you. God has birthed into you greatness, and you should embrace that walk with your head up."

I was stunned. "It's like you're reading my mind!"

Then I began to laugh. God knew I needed to hear those words. He chose to get that message to me through the most unlikely source I could imagine. Since then, I've liked Joel Osteen because God used his words to change my life and help me realize that I didn't have to listen to that condemning voice.

I spoke at that meeting with great freedom, and it turned out to be one of my best talks.

From that experience I learned two invaluable lessons.

First, it forced me to realize I needed to withhold judgment of people. Not knowing why, I had almost cut off Joel Osteen without giving him a chance.

Second, I learned that God will speak to us—and sometimes the answer may come in strange ways. But it will come. And a person we dislike very much might be the divine instrument He uses in our lives.

That second lesson is extremely important to me. At the Center for Fathering, I talk to many people and some of them have lived worse lives than I have. Some aren't easily liked, but I need to listen to them and feel their pain. I have to shake off that dirt and love them for who they are.

In doing so, I can offer them hope. I sometimes say, "I used to sell dope, but now I'm a *hope* dealer."

—————

A woman everyone called Sister came to the Center for Fathering in 2009, and told me, "I want to help people."

Those are words I like to hear, so I gave her a chance. But before long I realized how much help *she* needed. She seemed unaware of her own needs, but I saw promise in her and decided to do whatever I could.

We put her through our normal training programs and she did well. After that, Sister became the leader of the women's group. Because of her eager commitment, she became my female counterpart.

To be an effective group leader takes enormous drive and good communication skills. Even though it's a salaried position, the job requires as much as fourteen hours a day and the leaders must be fully devoted to Jesus.

One day, shortly before I married my current wife, Teresa, Sister said, "I'm in love with you."

"That's improper," I said. "We work together, and I don't allow any such relationships here."

"I understand," Sister said. But over the next few weeks, she made snide comments about Teresa to let me know she disapproved of my upcoming marriage. I ignored them, thinking she would get past that critical attitude.

To protect Sister and myself, I refused to travel out of state with her or do anything that anyone might consider improper. For several months, we worked well together, ministering to many people, and Sister did a fine job.

Then things changed. Imani, a former convict, became a Christian and started to work at the Center. He was good looking, six-foot-one, a powerful leader, and one of those individuals people just naturally like. He had gone into prison at age twenty, got out when he was thirty.

I mentored him carefully. Though I didn't tell Imani, he showed great promise. And I pegged him to be my successor.

Eventually, I realized that Sister was always following him around, as she had done with me just before she confessed her love. When I confronted her, she said, "I love Imani."

"He's twenty-five years younger than you are."

"I know. I want a strong man who can take care of me."

I couldn't demand that she stop caring for him, but I thought her obsession with him was unwise and unhealthy.

Before long, Imani told me he had fallen in love with Sister and wanted to marry her.

"One of you will have to leave the Center if you marry," I said, although he was aware of our policy.

"I know," he said, "and she's going to leave."

They married. After Sister left, she started her own organization and incorporated it. She persuaded every one of our women to go with her. She took all our teaching materials with her too. Even though that was illegal, we didn't try to get them back.

Within six months, Sister's program failed and she didn't have a client left.

Despite what Sister did, I never gave up on her. "I don't throw away friends," I told her. "I'm hurt and disappointed, but I'm going to love you the way I loved you when I met you."

I grieved even more over Imani, who also left the Center. Within months of marrying Sister, he realized that being married to a much older woman didn't work. After two years, they parted on good terms. Later, he became the husband of a lovely woman his own age.

"I'd like to come to work for you again," Sister said one day. "We did good things together. Give me a ministry. Help me rebuild and give me a platform."

Although I have genuine loving feelings toward her, when she asked I said, "No, I can't rehire you. You hurt the organization by the things you did and the awful things you said about the Center. I can't repair bridges outside my own personal ones."

Those were not easy words for me, but they were the right ones. I still pray for Sister and want to see her living successfully.

———

My worst disappointments are the people who start well, but then go back to their old ways. I don't want to ever give up on them, and more important, I don't want them to give up on themselves.

"You can remain faithful and strong," I tell people. "Jesus isn't partial. He won't do wonderful things for me but not for you."

The saddest failure, and the one closest to my heart, is that of Little Johnny. My son certainly didn't have any training for the good life from me. I've tried hard to make it up to him, but without much success.

While Little Johnny was incarcerated, I visited him and sent him books. He did read the Bible in prison.

In 2002, when Little Johnny got out of jail, I became involved in his life. He landed a job, and stopped selling drugs or even using them. I was happy and felt he had turned a corner and that God had answered my prayers. I even persuaded him to go to church a few times.

Then one day a friend told me that Little Johnny had started selling drugs again. I went by my son's house, and he didn't try to hide it from me. "Yeah, Dad, I'm dealing again."

His words broke my heart. I fell into a deep depression.

I questioned God. "You gave me a new life, so why can't You bring my son with me? Why couldn't You do for him what You did with me and get him out of this? Hasn't he suffered enough?"

I received no answer.

I tried to talk to Little Johnny many times, but it didn't seem to make a difference.

"Dad, this is my life." He wasn't angry, just honest.

I used to think of myself as a fixer. But that was the one thing I didn't know how to fix. I felt like a failure as a father, much as my own father had failed me.

———

Over the years, with my various girlfriends and wives, I fathered Lisa, Jamie, Tyray, and Demetrius. Along with Little Johnny, they all have father-absence wounds that I couldn't heal right away. At one point, I cried out to God, "I've been sober for five years. Please, please change them." God answered that prayer, but it took ten years.

Every night I think about my kids. During the day, I focus on other things, but at home in bed, I'm often tormented by my failure. One of the major reasons I changed was because I wanted to be a good dad to them—although it was too late and they didn't grasp what I was trying to do. Perhaps they were too shell-shocked because I hadn't had a good relationship with them for such a long time. They didn't trust me. And why would they? I had failed them far too often.

For years, those things haunted me. I even started to doubt my own new life and to feel I was a puny nothing.

35

SONS AND GRANDSONS

When my grandson Deaunteze Bobo was very young, his dad held him and his mom hostage with a knife to his mother's throat. He threatened to kill my stepdaughter Nikki and himself.

Little Johnny had dated Deaunteze's mother (who wasn't married to the father) and Deaunteze's father didn't want to lose her. That's why he came with a knife.

The police stormed in, and one of them shot Deaunteze's father in the forehead. The boy saw it happen and that memory damaged his life.

Little Johnny adopted the traumatized child, which was a loving gesture. And in 1990, he indoctrinated the young man into the gang life, with my unspoken blessings. I was still so messed up then, I thought it was cute to have a little gangbanger grandson. The pride of a thug's life is to have little thugs running around.

I had changed my life a couple of years before Little Johnny received a life sentence. When my son went to prison, I reached out to Deaunteze.

In spite of my efforts, Deaunteze walked in Little Johnny's footsteps. He went to County Home School, the first place all of us had gone. Then, like Little Johnny and me, Deaunteze graduated to Red Wing. So did his brother, Theadore, who was nicknamed Boo.

At age fifteen, Boo was shot in the chest by a rival gang because he belonged to our family. But he didn't die. That was the Turnipseed life.

After his time at Red Wing, I invited Deaunteze to the Center for Fathering. I gave him an internship, hoping to instill solid values into his life. In all honesty, it was mostly busy work, such as keeping the office in order. But I wanted him to be surrounded by good, strong men.

I didn't try to push him to go to church. Although I prayed that would happen, it's not my role to get people there. I often spend two or three years establishing a trusting relationship before I invite people to church. Deaunteze had been among gangs, where he was lied to, cheated, and deceived, so stable relationships weren't part of his life.

With Deaunteze, I reminded myself I'd probably only get one chance, and it had to be the right time.

"You mean you go to church every Sunday?" Deaunteze said to me one day.

"That's right. Every Sunday."

"What do you do there?"

"It's hard to explain. But you could come and see for yourself. We sing worship songs for the first fifteen minutes or so. But if you wait until ten forty-five or eleven o'clock to show up, you'll skip that part. And I promise you'll be out before the Viking game comes on."

"I'll think about it."

Two or three weeks later, he came to a Sunday service. When I asked how he liked it, he said it really didn't suit him. He admitted he liked the people, but they were mostly older, and the preacher didn't speak about things that Deaunteze found relevant. That didn't surprise me.

Deaunteze tried to do better, but Little Johnny kept dragging him back into the gang. By then, Little Johnny had created a gang with his kids.

But the curse is, they were part of the Turnipseed clan—related to me— and anywhere they went they were hunted. If they weren't in a gang, they had no protection. If they were, other family members had their back. Naturally, the gangbanger lifestyle was more appealing to them.

Although I knew about some of the robberies and other things Deaunteze and Little Johnny did, I was helpless to change them. All I could do was pray—which I did, daily and fervently.

In 2005, Deaunteze and Little Johnny robbed my stepson, Roamel, whom I had raised along with Little Johnny. Roamel had been selling a lot of drugs, and Little Johnny became angry. When Roamel showed him that he had $80,000, Little Johnny decided to rob him.

Not wanting Roamel to see him, Little Johnny took Deaunteze and two other relatives to do the job.

They waited outside Roamel's house until around three o'clock in the morning, when he came home. The two family members he didn't know held a gun on him and asked for his keys.

While they were growing up I had frequently told all my kids, "Do not let anyone take you into your house because once inside, they'll kill everybody. If you have to die outside the door, die outside the door. If they want your keys, throw them as far as you can," I said just as firmly, "just don't let them inside the house."

Remembering what I said, Roamel threw the keys as far as he could. That distracted the robbers. He took off running, but one of them tackled him.

Roamel didn't have the money on him, so they knew it had to be inside. But all our doors were fortified.

"We can't kick in the door," one of them said to the other, "so what we gonna do?"

Unable to figure out what to do, they took him to the car where Little Johnny and Deaunteze were hiding.

"We're family!" Roamel said when he saw his brother and Deaunteze. "What's going on here?"

"Now we're gonna have to kill you," Johnny said.

They took Roamel into the garage and demanded to know the location of the money. They stabbed him superficially three or four times so he would know they were serious. Knowing they would kill him no matter what he did, Roamel said, "It's in my stash house." The money wasn't really there, but the place had a security guard.

They believed Roamel, thrust him into the car, and took him to the house. A security guard with a gun questioned them. While they were distracted, Roamel ran away and was able to elude them.

Later, Roamel went to the hospital. Fortunately, none of the stab wounds were life-threatening.

When I got to the hospital, Roamel cried as he told me what happened. "My other brothers are going to kill Little Johnny and Deaunteze. And Little Johnny and Deaunteze might kill me."

I believed Roamel was trying to figure out if I truly loved him as much as I loved Little Johnny. And whether my new Christian lifestyle was real.

"You have to do what you have to do. But if you care about me, do me one favor."

He nodded and waited.

It wasn't easy for me, but I said, "Make them go to prison for what they did."

His eyes widened. "You want me to snitch on them?"

"It's not snitching if I tell you to do it. They'll probably have to do twenty years—"

"But snitching?"

"If you still feel the need to kill them once they're released, do it. But at least this will give you plenty of time to think about it."

The family never snitched on one another. But Roamel saw my reasoning. And he knew I loved him as well as Little Johnny and Deaunteze.

"Okay," he said.

Roamel told the police. He also put everything on Facebook and wrote, "Big Johnny said it's okay for me to turn in both of them."

Roamel's Facebook comment upset me because I felt it gave the wrong impression. I wasn't against my son and nephew, but I wanted to save their lives. But I couldn't change the Facebook post.

I went to see Little Johnny so I could explain why I wanted Roamel to tell the police. But before I got a chance, he said, "I hate that you told Roamel to turn us in. Why did you do that? Why'd you take his side against us?"

"I didn't take his side. But, Son, you were wrong. You tried to rob *your own brother!*"

"He ain't my real brother."

"I love all my kids . . . including you."

When he didn't answer immediately, I asked, "Why do you love Deaunteze?"

"I took him on as my stepson, and that means I agree to love him like he's my real kid."

"Now you understand how I feel. But you've had stepdads, and they didn't love you like their real son, did they? That hurt you. Right?"

"Yeah, but still . . ."

"Roamel is my son. You're also my son."

As we talked, I knew Little Johnny didn't understand—or maybe he chose not to.

"I want you to turn yourself in."

"Ain't gonna happen."

I felt depressed and helpless. "I want you to do this because I love you, and if you're in prison, you'll be safe."

"I ain't turnin' myself in, Dad."

I was caught in a rivalry between two sons who despised each other. Before I became a Christian I probably would have acted defiantly like Little Johnny and vengeful like Roamel. But I was different now. And that meant I acted different.

36

THE FAMILY DESTROYED

Despite my prayers to God and my pleas to both sons, nothing changed. Before long, word on the street was that Roamel had put out a hit on Little Johnny and Deaunteze for $50,000. I didn't know if that was true, but it might have been. Roamel had money; Little Johnny didn't.

Little Johnny was crazy—but again, his actions are what he had learned from me, his father. He didn't hide. He walked proudly around South Minneapolis.

Because he had only one leg and used crutches, he wasn't hard to find. One day, while he was standing on Broadway Street, two men shot him four times in the chest.

Someone called an ambulance and rushed Little Johnny to the hospital—a different one than before. As soon as I heard, I hurried over there.

After the surgery, the doctor came out to see me. To my surprise, it was the same woman who had operated when my son lost his leg.

"That kid must have a guardian angel," she said. "He should have died the last time. And he should have died this time too. But he's going to live."

I could hardly believe the news. I thanked her, and I thanked God. Each day that Little Johnny was alive, I would continue to pray for him and ask God to change his heart.

The surgeon said she expected him to be in the hospital for a couple of weeks. But a week later, Little Johnny called. "I'm doing real good, and my doctor says I can leave. Will you come and get me?"

That touched me. He'd been so angry with me and yet, when he needed a father, I was happy to be there for him. And grateful for another chance to make up for my many failures.

Roamel, or someone, finally turned Little Johnny in and the police issued a warrant for his arrest. But they decided to wait until he was discharged to pick him up.

When I arrived at the hospital, I discovered the doctor hadn't released him after all. "You lied, didn't you?"

Even as I asked the question, I understood his reasoning. He assumed Roamel's gang, and probably the police, would be waiting for him when the hospital discharged him. The solution, he decided, was to check himself out early.

I pleaded with him to stay until he was better.

He stared right at me and said, "I don't wanna go to jail."

Taking him out of the hospital without his doctor's authorization was illegal. But I had to put my son's life first. "Okay, I'll get you out of here."

I knew the gang wouldn't forfeit $50,000 by letting him go into police custody. So I took Little Johnny to a safe house, which no one knew about.

While he was convalescing, I got the expensive medication he needed through my family connections. I also provided him with food, and I brought some of his children to see him.

I wrestled with my conscience daily. I was breaking the law by shielding him. But if I didn't turn him in, some gangbanger would find out where he was and kill him.

One day, the lead officer from the City of Minneapolis's fugitive task force came to my office. He looked me right in the eye and said, "You say you're a minister now, and a good man. But have you really changed?"

Not sure how to respond, I said nothing.

"You're so loyal to your son, there's no way that you don't know where he is."

That police officer made me face the dilemma. I couldn't lie.

As I pondered how to answer, my own childhood flashed before me. My father had never been there for me when I needed him. But how could I be a follower of Jesus Christ and continue to hide Little Johnny?

"Give me one day," I said. "I need to make amends to my son before I turn him in."

Still staring at me, he measured my words, before he nodded. "All right."

After making sure I wasn't followed, I went to the safe house. When I went inside I saw Little Johnny lying on the couch with a puddle of blood underneath his body.

He's dying.

Little Johnny didn't care if he died. As a matter of fact, he wanted to go down like a big-time gangster. But I cared, and I couldn't let that happen. Tears filled my eyes, but I knew there was only one way I could keep Little Johnny alive and still live with myself. I walked into another room, picked up the phone, and called the police officer. I waited inside until I heard the sirens and then I left. I couldn't bear to see my son's disappointment in me.

Minutes later, Little Johnny called my cell phone. "The police are at my door."

Though the door was fortified, they could eventually break it down.

"I'm not giving myself up," he said. "If they come through that door they'll have to kill me."

"Son, I'll be right there. I'll call the officer and tell him to wait. When that door opens, I'll be standing there." I hung up before he could argue.

Before I had a chance to call the police, my cell rang again, and it was the officer in charge. "We're getting ready to—"

"Just wait! I'm on my way, and I'll open the door for you. Please! I'll be there within ten minutes."

"We'll wait for ten minutes. Not a second longer."

While I was with the gangs, many times I said in Little Johnny's presence, "Never call the cops. Die like a man." And now I was turning him over to the police. My own words mocked me.

When I arrived, the SWAT team was outside the house. I pulled out my keys. "I need to be the first one inside."

They stood back and let me go inside.

"Johnny, I'm here!"

When I walked into the room, I couldn't look him in the face. Even though I knew I had done the right thing, I had still betrayed him. My son would despise me even more. My only consolation was he would still be alive.

37

A GRAVE INJUSTICE

After I turned Little Johnny in, a string of things happened. Those who had been afraid of my son became bold. Within a short time, the inner circle of Little Johnny's gangbangers were all locked up on serious charges such as kidnapping, assault, and attempted murder.

Within a few days, Little Johnny, and his sons Deaunteze (whom they called De-nice) and Boo (Theodore), and my nephew called Lil Man were arrested. With those four out of circulation, the people who had been afraid of them were willing to testify. Roamel was the key witness against them.

The police convinced another family member named Tyson to turn state's evidence against Deaunteze for murder. All of them blamed me for their being in jail.

Most of the family, surprisingly, didn't consider me a snitch, at least not to my face; however, my grandsons were too angry to talk to me.*

Roamel was especially angry, accusing me of turning his sons against him. "Granddaddy put you in jail." He also said that if I hadn't made him turn Johnny in, Deaunteze Bobo wouldn't have received a life sentence.

That might be true, but it was the right thing. If I had it to do all over again, I would still do it. Although I don't know if I would do it exactly the same way, knowing it would lead to my grandson never being released.

---

* At the time of this writing, eight years later, all of my family members communicate with me, including my grandsons. I'm especially happy that Little Johnny and I now have a good relationship. Unfortunately, many of my male family members are incarcerated.

Little Johnny received a three-year sentence for the crime I turned him in for. But others also testified against him, so seven more years were added.

My nephew Lil Man is under a federal protection program and in prison somewhere out of state. I've tried, but have never been able to find out where he's imprisoned.

After those four went to prison, the CAN lost control of the neighborhood.

Those men were outlaws from the family gang. When Little Johnny got shot the first time in 1995, it was because the Bloods removed their protection. But now, gangs no longer come and go. In order to have power and spread fear, they have to be there all the time, enforcing their demands.

Everybody knew James Earl shot Little Johnny in 2005 when he lost his leg—that wasn't something that could have stayed a secret. Because the Bloods didn't stand behind him and retaliate, in Little Johnny's mind, he owed them no loyalty.

Little Johnny was arrested for a robbery gone bad where he, or one of his gang members, shot someone. The police finally caught Little Johnny after a high-speed chase.

When they questioned Little Johnny, he knew he couldn't beat the current charges, so he said, "Take it easy on me, and I'll give up three murders."

They agreed.

Little Johnny called me because he was under a $100,000 bail. It took ten percent of that for him to get out.

I had that much money, but I wasn't willing to give it to him.

When he was younger and I was still a career criminal, I would have done anything. But after I became a Christian, I told him repeatedly, "If you get in trouble, I'm not going to bail you out. You're selling dope and running through thousands of dollars a day. If you're silly enough not to put some away I'm not going to help."

The next day, however, Little Johnny got out of jail, and he came to see me. A detective was with him.

"Where did you get the money?" I asked.

"Didn't need it." After a long pause he said, "I'm turning state's evidence."

The detective said, "He wants your approval."

"I don't approve because he's doing it for the wrong reason." I looked the detective in the eye and said, "If *you* turned state's evidence, I'd approve because you have no motive for personal gain. You'd do it because you knew the person was guilty and it was the right thing to do. Being a civilian, it's okay."

I turned to Little Johnny. "But it's not right, Son, to get even by turning them in."

He started to object, but I raised my hand to stop him. "Why don't you wait until you get out of trouble and then come forward and say, 'To clear my conscience I'm going to tell on—'? And then tell on yourself too while you're doing it. That's the way I feel about it."

I turned back to the detective, and said, "I don't approve of what he's doing, but I will stand behind my son's decision and support him anyway."

And to this day, I still think he was wrong.

Before the day was over, I received a number of phone calls from family members, begging me to force Little Johnny to retract his testimony. Quite likely, I could have made Little Johnny do that, but I wouldn't. My son had made his decision and I was going to stand with him.

One of the police officers came to see me. "To turn state's evidence, Little Johnny will have to testify. The accused will have a chance to confront him; otherwise, it's just hearsay."

I understood how the system worked.

"We need you to make sure your son testifies."

"I'll stand by my son," I promised.

"You're *supposedly* a good man, and big in the community." From his tone of voice he made it clear that he didn't think I had changed.

"People make mistakes, but he's still my son."

I wished my own father had done something like that for me. If, just once, he had stood up for me, I wouldn't have gone through so many years of pain.

But now it was my turn, and I wouldn't fail my son.

———✁———

Little Johnny kept his word. Because of him, the police arrested several members of the Bloods. Two of them received life sentences.

They're all mad at him, and, to my knowledge, they still won't face the reality of their being guilty or wrong. To them, Little Johnny committed the ultimate act of betrayal: he informed on gang members.

The Bloods were a family gang, everyone was born into it, and they never snitched on each other. So that was the end of family reunions, which used to be huge. The split forced Turnipseeds to take sides. My brothers and I took my son's side and the rest of our clan treated us like outcasts. A once close-knit family had been destroyed.

———✁———

Faithfully, I visited Little Johnny in prison, and we were able to talk more heart-to-heart than we ever had before. He still held back, but I believe he knew I loved him and that he deserved to be in prison.

One time, as we were talking casually, Little Johnny dropped his head and was silent for a moment. I sensed he wanted to say something and I waited.

"Alonzo didn't commit the murder," he said in a low voice. "I lied about him."

I understood what my son was confessing. An out-of-state man visited our neighborhood and he was wearing a blue shirt. As one way to keep control, the Bloods didn't allow anyone to wear that color. Alonzo spotted the man, confronted him and said that in the Bloods territory, "You ain't supposed to wear blue."

"I'll wear whatever I want!" He brushed past Alonzo and walked on.

That much just about everyone in the community knew. Later that same day, the stranger was visiting in a home. Someone, standing outside, shot through the window and killed him.

No one admitted having seen the shooter, although many of us assumed Alonzo had killed him. Because of Little Johnny's testimony, my cousin, Alonzo, was convicted and sentenced to prison for life.

"You need to make this right," I said.

My son only nodded.

The next day, I visited Alonzo's lawyer. "My son lied about your client." He couldn't believe it, but I gave him the details that Little Johnny had told me. Because of my testimony, Alonzo received a new trial.

I felt terrible that my son had committed perjury, and that I testified against him. But I had to do it.

At the trial, Little Johnny wouldn't say anything. He pleaded the Fifth Amendment, which says that no one can be forced to self-incriminate. What it meant to the jury, however, was that Little Johnny had lied.

At the trial, the judge said, "John Turnipseed has too much to lose by lying. He could lose his reputation, his new life, and his son. That's why I believe him."

That statement was encouraging, and I should have been overjoyed. But I was miserable. No matter what I did, I displeased somebody.

Art assured me that even though I was caught between the proverbial rock and a hard place, I had done the right thing.

The judge overturned my cousin's life sentence. That case became one of the most cited cases in Minnesota history. Other lawyers use it to get hearsay evidence into a trial because never before had that been allowed.

—⁓—

Even without my son's testimony, they tried Alonzo three times. They convicted Alonzo the third time, and he received a sentence of twenty years as opposed to life.

Alonzo was innocent that time, but he was guilty of a number of other things.

I've been using what influence I have, and he'll get out soon. I've been hoping that my intervention might repair my relationship with family members who were against me, but it hasn't—at least not so far. They respect me and wouldn't do anything to me, but they would still hurt my son if they could.

I suspect they will try to kill Little Johnny when he gets out in

2016, unless he leaves the state. I know it, and he knows it. But he probably won't leave because his attitude seems to say, "I don't care."

One time he told me, "When they shot off my leg they took my life." That's why he refuses to hide.

I pray daily that Little Johnny will change. And he has changed a lot. He's articulate and a good speaker. If he becomes a believer, I'd love to go on tour with him so we can talk about our relationship and the changes and challenges we went through. I love him and want to keep him close.

I've heard him speak in front of kids. They're fascinated by a one-legged man who is tough as nails, and despite everything, Little Johnny has a big heart.

I've assumed custody of his youngest son and I'm trying to shower on him the affection and attention I didn't give his dad and I didn't get from my own father.

38

A FEW MORE FACTS

At the Center for Fathering, we had ten people the first year I was in charge. Soon we had fifty, then seventy-five, and we continue to grow. Not everyone stays with the program, although most of them do. Some have stayed in the group for five years.

The government now recognizes what we're doing and we're receiving federal grants that help us further reach into the community.

I know God is using everything in my past to make a new way for me. I'm grateful that He has been using me as an example of transformation. That's a high honor.

As I said at the beginning of this book, I should be dead by now. Starting with that unfulfilled father wound, I went in the wrong direction most of my life. And then God stepped in.

I've been amazed at how God has worked in my life. My story was on TV and it received an Emmy award. I got to meet the Dalai Lama (a great story for another book). Several times I've been in conferences with high-level government officials. That's God's grace in my life.

I never had a father who expressed any love or acceptance, and I felt worthless. That is, until I became a Christian. From feeling worthless and like scum, now I *know* I am equal to every person God has ever put on this earth. Some are much wiser than I am, and others are harder workers. But I, at least, can be on the same field as they are in God's sight.

Through all of this, my mom, Earlene Turnipseed, has been a big supporter. After I stopped my dad from hitting her when I was in my teens, she and I became close friends. She's nearly eighty years old now and still a strong, opinionated woman.

But my mother has always believed in God and prayer. She has remained the one constant in my life. I refer to myself as a momma's boy because my mother has loved me unconditionally. Regardless, she's argued with her sisters and even called them names whenever they've said bad things about me.

"Lene, that boy's going to be the death of you," I overheard one sister say. "You need to stop worrying and just forget about him. Don't let him back in your house, he's just bad."

And my mom would get very angry and tell them, "That's my son."

The only time she was un-Christian-like was when someone attacked her kids. She took care of us and always had a place for us to stay. I could lie on my mom's floor and sleep for twenty days if I needed to and she'd be happy.

Mom raised two of my daughters, Jaime and my oldest child, Lisa. Tyray is the youngest of my still-living children. Then I have Dee Dee, short for Demetrius, and Little Johnny.

I made bad decisions with many women, including three wives, before I became a Christian. The fifth time I finally got it right when I married Teresa in 2005. We were both Christians serving Jesus Christ."*

I met Teresa when she was fifteen and I was twenty. She was beautiful, mature beyond her age, and street savvy. I knew she had a crush on me, but I didn't go out with her because she was too young. (If she had been twenty years old when we met, I think she truly would have been the one and lasting love of my life.)

We went our separate ways, but over the years, we saw each other from time to time. She always asked, "Are you married?" And every time I was. Teresa had rigorous standards against messing with married men.

Once I became a Christian, I didn't fool around; when I was married, I was really married.

Before Teresa became a Christian she owned a drug house—a place

---

* Although I haven't gone into detail about other marriages and children, I've raised three stepsons, Tony, Roamel, and Mandel. I have twenty-nine grandkids and three great-grandkids.

where people could come and buy drugs and stay as long as they could afford to keep sniffing or mainlining. Because Teresa wasn't strung out on drugs herself, she managed the house well. I admired that about her. She dabbled in drugs, but I never saw her get high—that would have made her vulnerable to what I called the alligators.

Teresa was stunningly beautiful, and a great hustler. She had a nice little racket going. She enticed men, and when she got them into her room, she robbed them.

Often, Teresa's scams were more complex. She would team up with men and women from the streets in an endeavor to make money off some rich, unsuspecting stranger.

First, she would linger on the outskirts of a parking lot at a big corporate building where white males might be looking for a woman to hook up with. After some small talk, she'd ask him for a ride home in his big, fancy car.

When the guy pulled up to the curb in our neighborhood, Teresa would climb out and give everyone a subtle signal to alert us that she wanted the man robbed. The signal might be something like waving to someone in a passing car.

Black guys were too dangerous to trick because they could come back into the neighborhood. We might not remember them, but they would remember and hurt us.

We had houses where women like Teresa could take rich johns. Once inside Teresa slowly undressed. Before she became fully naked, an "angry husband" slammed open the door, rushed in, and pointed a gun at the guy. "What are you doing with my wife?"

The poor white man was always scared to death. He knew if he got shot, the news reports would say he was shot while fooling around with another man's wife. So his only question was, How do I get out of this?

The man would start apologizing. "I didn't know she was married."

The "angry husband" demanded the man empty his pockets before he let him out of there. If the john had a nice car, the husband made him leave on foot, then drove his car to Chicago, about eight hours away. After partying for a few days, the husband abandoned the car.

It was a dangerous way to make a living, and there were a couple of mishaps.

A female cousin of mine was a streetwalker. She and her boyfriend tried to rob a trick who turned out to be an undercover police officer. The cop pulled his .45 Magnum, the boyfriend grabbed it. In the struggle, the officer and the boyfriend were shot. Both lived, but my cousin could have been killed.

Then the Latinos moved in and invaded our territory. We soon discovered they were paid on Fridays. Since they didn't like banks, they kept their money in their pockets. So they seemed like easy targets.

One of my friends tried to rob a Latino with the angry-husband trick, but the Latino cut his throat and left him for dead. However, my friend survived.

Of course, everything depended on what type of prostitutes we had out working. If we had straight flat-backers, as we called them, they turned a date for twenty or twenty-five dollars. Nobody was allowed to rob them because they'd become regular customers. We might get a hundred tricks coming through a night.

Of course, that amount could escalate to hundreds of dollars, if we could get the johns to start smoking dope. The dope man was always right there and ready.

Some buddies and I rented an apartment and fixed it up with everything a trick might want, where they could come back as many times as they wanted and feel safe.

But we had to watch out for police. We knew the vice squad only worked from eight in the evening until two in the morning. So from eight to two, the girls would work strip clubs or massage parlors.

Our best street traffic was in the early, early morning, as well as between two and four in the afternoon. Believe it or not, four or five in the afternoon was actually the most lucrative time. Any man coming down the street alone during those hours was generally looking for drugs or a woman. Or both.

The vice squad was made up of black men who were dressed like us. But because we knew our neighborhood, a new man was at a disadvantage. And once an undercover agent busted one of the girls, he couldn't come back.

Because we knew the difference by their cars and clothes, we robbed only the very high-end tricks who generally wanted women like Teresa: wholesome-looking, well manicured, wearing nice jeans and blouses, not in high heels or tight-fitting clothes.

These women didn't turn twenty-five-dollar tricks. They would tell the men it cost $500 or $600 because they were cleaner, prettier, and younger than the others.

Certain tricks would pay that amount of money. But they usually went to massage parlors, where they knew nobody would rob them. Our district had several massage parlors. After all, our neighborhood was a sex district.

After a few years, Teresa changed her life and became an entrepreneur. She bought a daycare and owned several properties.

I lost track of Teresa after I became a Christian and turned my life around. But in October 2003, a year or so after Maury and I split, I was working at the Center when Teresa brought in a young woman who needed help.

Just then the woman said, "You ain't got a man and that guy over there is divorced. You guys would make a great couple."

When Teresa recognized me, we started talking. She invited me to go for coffee. After she realized the change in me, she told me that she too had become a believer.

"I'm still married," I said. That really was a lie, but I was playing her off just to see if she was serious. "Come see me in about six months."

"Where?"

"Come to my office at five o'clock." I told her to come on February 13, which was Little Johnny's birthday. I didn't expect to see her again.

At exactly five o'clock, six months later, she showed up at my office. We had each come from really terrible backgrounds and Jesus Christ had changed us both. We started dating and eighteen months later, we married and have stayed married.

Before we met, she had been sick with sarcoidosis, but it was in remission. For most people that's the end of it and the sarcoidosis doesn't recur. One medical man said, "It's like muscular dystrophy on steroids." When the disease first appeared, she became paralyzed for six months, and it destroyed the sight in her right eye.

"I thought I was down for the count," she told me. She recovered fully except the vision in her eye.

39

A CHANGED MAN

Here's a story about Elmer that shows the way I've changed. I'd known Elmer, who was related to my former wife, since he was a kid. Although he wasn't a blood relative, he had always respected me. And called me Uncle.

I had helped him out of situations and took an interest in him as if he were my own son. Then I learned he was pimping out two of my cousins who were sisters. When he started messing with another one of my cousins, I felt he was running through my family like they were toilet paper. That's how pimps operate—they have no morals. They often pimped mothers along with their daughters.

But I had changed by the time I married Teresa. I owned a six-bedroom house and only the two of us lived there. We lived in the gang- and drug-infested territory north of the Bloods gang. But the kids there knew who I was, so they wouldn't break into my house, and Teresa felt safe.

In 2010, new kids moved into the community and a group of them tried a home invasion. They'd heard that I was an old gangster who wore suits every day and had two nice shiny cars. Because I owned a hundred-pound dog, they didn't get inside, but it was enough to alarm my wife.

Because Teresa felt unsafe, we were just going to sell the house. I talked to the bank and said, "It's hard to sell, but we've got to leave here. My wife refuses to be here by herself. She doesn't want anybody else living with us." I already had a buyer, but it was going to take four months to sell the house. So the bank and I made an agreement.

We wanted to move out immediately, but if the house was empty, people could come in and strip the copper or anything else they could resell.

So Teresa talked me into letting Elmer and his son, Roan, move in. Roan was a kid I had once saved from a kidnapping charge, so I assumed they would be loyal and not take advantage of me.

"We'll charge him a small rent and get him to watch the house," I told my wife. She agreed.

Elmer and Roan lived there for a time. My first deal fell through because the buyer couldn't come up with the finances. The second buyer, along with the real estate agent, came to see the house, but Elmer wouldn't let them inside. Other prospective buyers came and the same thing happened.

Elmer had a great deal—big house and cheap rent—so he didn't want me to sell and was willing to do anything he could to stop it. Later, I found out that he also rented out four bedrooms and made money out of the property.

After I discovered Elmer was refusing to let them in, I made sure people got to see inside. Finally, I sold the house and on the day before closing the buyer wanted a final walk-through, but Elmer wouldn't let him inside.

The buyer called me, and I went over and said to Elmer, "You have to get out of here and let these people in. And then you have to move out."

"I'm not going anywhere."

Roan pulled a knife on me.

I didn't say much, but I left. In the old days I would have taken care of both of them. Instead, I called my five brothers and they met me at the house. I didn't let them do anything to Elmer, but I wanted to show him that I wasn't going to be intimidated. "I'm going to call the police on you," I said.

But he picked up the phone and called the police on me. They came and made me leave because I didn't have any paperwork evicting him. He proved that he lived there and received mail at that address.

I didn't know the rental rules. As I learned, in Minnesota, if a person gets mail where they're living, they can't be put out without going to court and having them evicted. That takes two or three months. (Elmer had done it to someone else, which is how he knew.)

Some of my relatives, people still loyal to me, said, "If you want him out of there we'll get him out." It wouldn't have been a problem, but the way they would use to get him out was a problem in my new life. And Elmer knew that.

It was a struggle, but I surrendered to God and told them, "Thanks, but don't do anything."

But occasionally people came to me and said, "Elmer has turned it into a crack house."

Elmer bragged to everyone. "Johnny Turnipseed is a Christian now. He won't do nothin', so I don't gotta worry about him."

Before I became a Christian, just my stepping into the house would have put such fear in Elmer that he would have run out of there. I had zero tolerance. He knew that nobody in my adult life ever refused me anything that I asked.

I didn't have to take beatings and don't have many scars on my body because everyone knew I anticipated opposition. I wasn't interested in just giving black eyes and broken bones. Instead, I would strike first, intimidate them, and make sure they never troubled me again.

Getting shot once or twice in our life is normal for the successful ones. Some of the people I knew had been shot twenty or thirty times and their lives are always in danger.

The end of the story with Elmer is that eventually he was evicted by the bank. A number of my old friends said to me, "I couldn't have handled it the way you did." Because they knew the old John Turnipseed, they realized I had a tremendous amount of integrity to let that happen the way I did.

I didn't give in joyfully and had to fight myself all the way, but I knew I did the right thing. God honored my decision because people came to me who hadn't believed in my conversion. Those naysayers in that world I came from, are now believers. My actions also brought three or four clients who needed and wanted help. They came because they realized I had a forgiving heart and I was a changed man.

40

A LETTER FROM JOHNNY

L ittle Johnny sent me a letter from prison. Of all the letters I've ever
received, this is the one closest to my heart.*

I decided to write this letter to let someone know how I've been
feeling since childhood. And I couldn't think of a better person
than you, so please forgive me if I become a little emotional.

Ever since I could remember, probably at the age of nine or ten
years old, I have been struggling to find my place in life, due to what
I endured living with my mother and grandmother. It seemed to me
that life was more difficult for me than for the rest of the kids. Out
of a dozen kids that lived with me at my Grandmother Edwards's
house, I was the only kid who was teased and talked about.

My older cousins and the ones my age ridiculed me because of
my different colored face, (which is half-green because of a birth
defect) and talked about my eyes because they are bigger than
most people's. They called me names like bubble eyes, guppy, fish
eyes, frog eyes, ugly, and more names than I care to remember.

They made me feel I was out of place for being there among
the normal, or what they considered the normal. What they didn't
know is they were teaching me how to hate myself and others. I
started hating what I did not like, including myself.

At the age of twelve or thirteen, I began stealing cars, clothes,
and money from my friends' parents—never my own parents—
because I had the utmost respect for you and Mom, no matter how
she treated me, and how much you weren't in my life. Mom would

---

* I have edited this slightly.

whip me and talk about my eyes and my darker color because I was darker than Lisa, Dee, and Jamie.

When I tried to talk to her or ask her something she would say, "Get out of my face!" I remember her handing me to Aunt Nelva and giving cousin Coco every last bit of her love like I wasn't even her child, and telling Coco to ask you for stuff when you came to see me and Lisa. You would give him money, not knowing it was killing me on the inside.

I used to ask Mom to rent me a football uniform so I could play for Powder Horn Park, or if she would buy me name brand shoes, or clothes, and she would say, "Call your daddy."

She tried to turn me against the one person I felt really loved me—you—but I never would.

You both were drug users and alcoholics, so I would never ask for anything really big after that. I began trying to kill myself, not with my own hands but, by doing things to people that would make them kill me, like robbing or beating them. I beat women the same way I saw men beat up my mom.

This lifestyle made me feel equal and sometimes more powerful than God or the Devil. I began carrying guns every day and looking for trouble, and I found plenty of it running with the Bloods, our own family.

As years went by, my violence increased to a deadly stage to where my own family got scared of me themselves and they were older than I was. Soon everyone around me liked me because I would protect them, but also they didn't trust me because I was devious and hateful.

I started getting into it with people. When they shot me up in a setup, I really didn't care about dying, but I said to myself I would get them back just because they tried to kill me. I didn't succeed because they persuaded my own family and friends to help them. I got them back by sending them to jail. That is the only thing I regret in my life—going to the police and I did that only because I figured I would never be able to kill all of them. I only feel bad because I am not a rat and I don't tell on people. That was the only time.

I began robbing dope dealers and not caring. I married Linda just to have someone around me to trust because I was burning a lot of bridges. I did not care because I knew that I had you, no matter what happened. When I went to prison the first time, I knew that nobody would be around but you, so it was easy time. I tried to learn to love myself while locked up, and I almost succeeded but there was one piece of the puzzle missing—my leg—and I knew I could never rest until I was dead or all of them were dead.

When I got to the halfway house something would not let me leave. I really wanted to. I was kind of upset because I didn't understand your reasoning of what went on with Roamel because I would rather be dead than in prison, after all, I was looking for death because I didn't want to live any longer. When you told me what you told Roamel to do about me and his situation, I never said anything to you about it because I didn't know how to tell you that you hurt me. I never had to tell you that before. When you asked me to go to that retreat for the weekend with you I said yes because I figured that we could talk about how I felt, but we never did. And I can tell you why. That weekend I realized I was in a no-stress situation and with one of the most important people in my life besides God—that was you, Dad. Without words God let me know right then and there that I was trying to die but you were trying to keep me alive because you loved me.

You did what a person does when they care and love someone special to them and right then I realized I really had something to live for besides my wife and kids. It's you, Dad. I know now that you love me more than I loved myself. All because of that weekend we spent together with God. I can really say I want to live; I don't want to die. I think this is the beginning to finding the Lord and myself.

I owe you most of the credit for caring enough to keep me alive to love myself and my loved ones around me.

I love you, Dad.

41

FINAL THOUGHTS

Despite my first forty years of criminal activity, failure, and sin, the last twenty years have reversed that. God forgave me and wiped away the past. I owed much more than I could ever repay, but God honored my faithfulness and picked up the tab for all my debts.

One of the reasons I wrote this book was to offer hope. Too many of us carry what we sometimes call *the father wound* because we didn't feel the love of a father while we were growing up. I've dedicated my life to showing men how to overcome the pain of childhood. At the Center for Fathering, we want to build strong families and help members love and strengthen each other.

The greatest lesson I've learned as a Christian is to accept God's loving forgiveness—something I couldn't earn and didn't deserve. Once I received His forgiveness, I was able to forgive myself for the hurt I've caused others. I can also forgive those who have wronged me.

Even more, I've learned to look for the best in everyone, regardless of their circumstances. I'm convinced that there's some good in everyone. We may have to dig deeply to find that goodness, but it's there.

When I'm tempted to give up on someone, I remember that most people thought I was bad, worthless, and hopeless. And I didn't blame them, because I felt the same way about myself. Despite that, a handful of faithful, loving people sought the good in me, prayed faithfully for me, talked to me, and refused to give up.

In 1994, I quit robbing people and businesses, pimping, selling and using drugs, and gave up my way of life as a gangbanger. That's when

I finally stopped fighting God, listened to the loving counsel of caring people, and started my new life in Christ.

Since then, my life has been greatly blessed, which is the major reason I've shared the story of my redemption. I want to give hope to those who feel they're not good enough for God and want to give up on themselves. If God delivered me out of such a destructive life—He can do the same for anyone.

Changing my life seemed impossible, but I've proven it can—and did—happen. Once, negative influences filled my life. Prison or hell seemed my only option; I was without hope. But after I turned to Jesus Christ, everything in my life was different.

God saved me from crime and from myself. I've been changed so that I can reach out to others and show them that our loving God refuses to abandon anyone.

———

As I write this, I think of the second chance I got—many second chances. Finally, I faced what was truly my last chance, and had to decide whether to continue down the same road or change directions. I was so desperate I could only fall on my face and cry out to God.

I got it right only because I couldn't run anymore. Once I changed direction, God not only forgave me, but that's when I realized He had a plan for my life—a plan that no one else could fulfill but John Turnipseed. And it's the same with all of us—we're miserable until we lovingly turn to God's wonderful, surprising, and all-loving plans for us.

For a long time I was an evil person; however, God "so loved the world," and that amazing love included John Turnipseed. That made me face that I'm important to God. And each of us *is* important. After that, I was able to start becoming the man I am today—one who cares and reaches out to others who need a second chance—or a tenth chance.

———

Another thing I want to emphasize is hope. Without sensing something worthwhile is possible, nothing improves. Why work on a car that we know will never run again? I believe everyone is born with hope, but negative conditions destroy our expectations and make many of us feel worthless. And if we feel worthless, we treat others as being as bad as we are.

That hopelessness showed itself not only in the way I treated others, but also in my struggles with depression and feeling life had no purpose or meaning.

That day in my office when I fell on the floor, I hit bottom with nowhere else to go. That was the beginning of true hope—sensing that the Lord loved me and wanted to set me free. In that miserable condition, I reached out to God and He clasped my hand. Slowly, I began to accept that I might be worth something.

My new life began with transformation. The apostle Paul says that if we're in Christ, all things become new.* Yet we can't be new creatures and still live the way we did in the past. Although the transformation may be hard and painful—at least it was for me—it was the best thing I ever did.

Most of us don't willingly choose a spiritual makeover; it chooses us. When God came into my life, He transformed me, stayed with me, encouraged me, and forgave me when I failed. When I want to give up, even now, Jesus whispers. "I . . . chose you and appointed you so that you might go and bear fruit—fruit that will last."**

Since that day in 1994, I've been involved in a spiritual "renovation." That journey freed me to head toward where I should have been in the first place.

But be aware: There's a cost involved—we can't remain who we were. Transformation means we first must be broken, torn down, and then slowly rebuilt.

My transformation went into effect when I repented. Scholars tell us the Greek word for repent means to turn around, and when we repent, God turns us in a new direction. We forsake the old ways because we've discovered a new and better way—a life of peace and joy.

I also want to point out two significant life principles—among many which stand out for me since I've become a disciple of Jesus Christ.

---

*   See 2 Corinthians 5:17.
** John 15:16.

The first life principle I can sum up in the word *loyalty*. Nothing can interfere with good decisions quite like loyalty, especially when we give it to the wrong people. Loyalty built on guilt, fear, or need can ruin not only households but also whole communities. My gangbanger days with the Bloods showed that.

Immediately, I think of my dad. As violent and destructive as my father was, I remained loyal to him for a long time. I could have called the police on him. I should have, but I didn't. In spite of everything, I loved him. Right or wrong, he had my loyalty. And that's what makes loyalty so potentially dangerous. Loyalty can hinder us from doing what we're supposed to do. We hide behind that devotion so we don't have to examine how we feel or whether we're doing the right thing.

I think of Little Johnny's ordeal. After his best friend accidentally shot a family member, the Bloods ordered my son to kill that friend. He couldn't do it so he refused. His allegiance to a friend blinded him to everything else.

As I see it, Little Johnny's commitment to the family was based mostly on evil influence (which started with me), coercion, and guilt. As powerful as his negative loyalty was, his commitment to a friend was stronger. Or another way to say it is that my son loved his friend more than he was devoted to the demands of the gang.

This much I've learned about true loyalty: It's never coerced but must be freely given. Fear or intimidation may bring conformity and obedience, but that's not the same as loyalty.

The best example of loyalty is Jesus' total self-giving to His heavenly Father. Jesus' life and death were freely given and He knew He would die for the benefit of all humanity.

In return for His love, Jesus asks for our loyalty. We can use many words such as trust, commitment, dedication, allegiance, or faithfulness, but loyalty covers them. False or forced loyalty comes and goes with our needs and our wants, but true loyalty is unshakeable and unbreakable love. And love always does the right thing.

The second life principle revolves around the *family*. Those who don't value their families won't truly have one. And those without families are missing out on the essentials of life. My family is the root of everything; it's my lifeblood. But it wasn't always that way.

As a child, I needed a strong family, but instead of caring for me and being a positive influence, they scarred me. Despite the godly influence of my mother, the bigger family of my bloodline pulled me away. They didn't protect me or give me hope. They weren't truly family—only blood relatives.

Once I started my own family, I repeated the negative things I'd learned. I had nothing to build on. For the first two-thirds of my life, I was submerged in a culture where nobody had real families, and my negative influence destroyed my sons. It wasn't until I was forty-five years old that I started to understand the true meaning of family.

My toughest job is to continue to live up to the standard Jesus set for me when He commanded all disciples to love God with all our hearts and our neighbors as ourselves.* But that task is also rewarding—because He gives us the Holy Spirit to guide us and empower us. We have the Bible and prayer and the help of other believers who have gone through the painful places we're facing.

I still struggle with fears and doubts, but deep inside, I know everything will be all right. Even when things don't go the way I want, I'm able to believe they're going the way they're supposed to go.

I've devoted my life to helping others—and I refuse to give up on them. Because of my past, I'm able to reach those that others pass by, ignore, or look down on. I can't give up on them, because God never gave up on me.

That's the best news of all: God hasn't given up on any of us.

Not anyone.

Not me.

Not you.

---

* See Matthew 24:37–39.

NOW WHAT DO I DO?

By Art Erickson,
Co-founder of Urban Ventures and Mentor to John Turnipseed

A wise friend once said that all the best stories end with a question: "So what?" You have read about the transformed life of John Turnipseed. So what about your life?

Everybody is surrounded by people who want to write the script of our lives for us, to edit our story, to change our identity, or to make us a bit player in their story. Like John did, we hope you will take this opportunity to take back the pen and write your own story.

Jesus Christ came to seek out and to save the least, lost, last, and left out. How did you get lost? It happens in a million different ways. The issue is not really what has happened to us, but what we do with what has happened to us.

Because of all God's intentional work in creating us just right, His great love causes Him to chase us down the streets and the alleys, through our crimes, into the cell blocks, and right into the core of our lives—hoping we will turn around to see His caring, forgiving, and loving face. He wants you to hear Him ask, "Do you know that I love you?"

Then He wants us to get on with the script He wrote for our lives and to write it with Him. But God never forces His plan on anyone. The only way to get it is to choose.

Jesus' love is reaching out for you with the simple question: "So what?" Take Jesus' hand, pray, and begin to walk into your own amazing, world-changing story.

Are you ready to make the choice for starting your relationship with God through Jesus Christ that lasts for eternity? Below are words to consider carefully. When you are ready, pray them on your knees and from the depths of your heart:

"Heavenly Father, I want you to be the Father I can really know and respect. I know you have always loved me, and I respect Your plan for my life. You understand all the pain and violence of my world, and love me anyway. Lord Jesus, I need You. Thank You for dying on the cross for me. I open the door of my life and receive You as my Savior and Lord. I confess all my many sins to You and thank You for forgiving my sins and now giving me eternal life. Take control of the very center and throne of my life. Make me the kind of person You want me to be."

You have just finished reading the amazing story of a man who prayed a prayer like this, and the whole world around him changed. If you just prayed this prayer, you have begun a new relationship with God The Father through Jesus Christ. It's time to start your amazing story.

If you would like more information or to reach John Turnipseed, please see his contact information on the About the Authors page.

—ART ERICKSON
StudiOne-Eighty, Urban Ventures

ACKNOWLEDGMENTS

AB and Earlene Turnipseed and the Turnipseed-Dower-Berry Family. You are my family and I love you.

With love to my children Lisa, Johnny, Shaun, Dee, Jamie, and Tyray, and to my brothers Isaiah, Sterling, Michael, Jerome, Darryl, Markalow, and my sister, Bonita.

Teresa Jackson-Turnipseed: because you are truly special to me.

To my twenty-eight grandchildren, I love all of you, as well as my stepsons, Mandel, Tony, and Roamel Dalton.

To all of my nineteen aunties, I love you.

Helen Ferguson, you're very important in our family history.

I send this book out in memory of Kay Eason and Maury Latzer.

Other special people I want to acknowledge include Niko Hall, Sheron Edwards, Cydnae Anderson, Teresa Dalton, Jennifer Sonnee, Nikki Lee, and Trina Dalton.

Each day I give thanks for the vision and people involved with Urban Ventures Leadership Foundation.

Where would I be today if it hadn't been for my three mentor-father figures? Thank you Art Erickson, Father Capoochi, and Dan Taylor.

And right along with that, my grateful acknowledgment to Amicus. Your staff opened their arms to me when I wasn't worthy of acceptance or help. But you did it anyway.

I don't want to forget Carey Casey of the National Center for Fathering. Thank you, Carey, for your influence.

I can't overlook Awaken Films and Erwin Mcmanus and the Five Stone Media family, especially Steven Johnson. Steve, you kept this vision alive. God bless you. You have been a blessing to all of us.

Really special thanks to Dave Logan who believed in the project from the beginning.

Thanks to Jimmy Duke and friends.

MADDADS and VJ Smith, and you know you're special to me.

Volunteers of America, thank you for what you do for the world.

My appreciation to my brother-in-law, Darrin Wallace; Mayor Betsy Hodges; Gary Cunningham; Billy Hawkins; Sister Retha; Imani Coble; Ruth Johnson; and Eddie Santiago.

I send a big shout out to the one and only Jack Strawder who is still struggling. May our Father continue to bless you.

I also want to acknowledge the influence in my life by Jackie Whitmore, Sherrie Strawder, Larry Gillard, Gill Baggett, Alfonso Mayfield, Gloria Howard, Stan Hill, Viani Torres, Romericus (Sarge) Simms, Josh Shelton, Don Constable, Mary Ferguson, Emma Ferguson, Gary Boatwright, Tony Potberg, Patrick Baggett, Beth Becker, Ann Heron, Judy Jones, Frankie and Velma Tyson, Julie Grengs, Carol and Frank Wooten, Marv and Ganis Greener, Mark Bierle, Heidi Habben, Heidi Stokes, Kara Johnson, Mike Johnson, Nate Jameson, Ricky Grandsberry, Joseph Kling, Judy Wright, Kathy Erickson, Jimmy Kennedy, Joe Edwards, Robert Edwards, Jim Bransford, Billy Richardson, Earnest Coleman, Warren and Kevin Johnson, Alan Eastman, Mark Peter Lunquist, Governor Al Quie, Sheriff Rick Stanek, Dan Cain at RS Eden, and Doctor Hayden at Turning Point, Matt Vonende, Susanna Desugula Espinoza, Dan Lamberdies, Beth Becker, Paul Wright, Darlene Kilgore, Willie Kilgore, Nelva Loyd, Elainer Ferguson, Tommy Ferguson, Jimmy Ferguson, and Pastor Greg Bauldwin.

Although others are too many to name, I'm grateful to all the special people who've supported me and loved me through all of this.

And finally, to my co-writer, Cecil Murphey, and to my publisher, Carlton Garborg, who brought this idea to an excellent reality.

ABOUT THE AUTHORS

JOHN TURNIPSEED, a former gang leader and drug dealer, is a community leader, pastor, speaker, facilitator, and has written parenting curriculum. For more than fifteen years, John was the director of the Center for Fathering at Urban Ventures in Minneapolis, Minnesota, and was promoted to vice president in 2014. Overcoming the deadly effects of a violent, absent father and the downward spiral of gang life, John is passionate about helping rebuild relationships and successful living.

Please use the contact information below to contact John.

Five Stone Media
PO Box 667
Hugo, MN 55038
612-787-7172
www.fivestonemedia.com

CECIL MURPHEY has written or cowritten more than 135 books, including the *New York Times* bestseller *90 Minutes in Heaven* (with Don Piper) and *Gifted Hands: The Ben Carson Story* (with Dr. Ben Carson). His books have sold in the millions and have brought hope and encouragement to countless people around the world.

RESOURCES FOR HELP AND HOPE

www.urbanventures.org/turnipseed-bloodline

Call: 612-638-1024

(Special number for readers of this book)

E-mail: johnturnipseedbloodline@urbanventures.org

The website above contains contact information of partners and friends who can help you find the hope you're looking for. These organizations include Urban Ventures, Leadership Foundations, National Center for Fathering, Navigators, Prison Fellowship, Salvation Army, World Impact-TUMI, and others.

For more about John Turnipseed's life, order three award-winning short films *Turnipseed*, *Second Chance*, and *Legacy* available at

www.fivestonemedia.com

Also available from Five Stone Media is *LifeBlood*, a follow-up character curriculum video series highlighting the following character traits: family, influence, hope, power, self-reliance, second chances, loyalty, the right thing, and transformation. The nine steps in *Lifeblood* will unearth root issues affecting your ability to live free. Comes with a facilitator's guide.